Praise for
BREATHING

"Ministry is hard work. It's spiritually draining, emotionally taxing, and intellectually exhausting. Josh opens his heart and shares the pain most leaders carry but reveal to no one. It becomes the secret burden we endure until something breaks. *Breathing Room* will reveal the warning signs that we're headed towards a crash, but gives us hope that healthy living is possible for those of us in church work."

—**Bob Franquiz,** senior pastor, Calvary Fellowship, founder,
Church Ninja

"While there may be no such thing as a stress-free life, the stress-dominated life has almost become the norm in our modern-day culture. In his new book, *Breathing Room,* Josh Reich exposes the most common sources of crippling stress and lays out a game plan for conquering the beast that so easily robs our joy and sabotages our walk with Jesus."

—**Larry Osborne,** author and pastor, North Coast Church

"In *Breathing Room,* Josh Reich opens up with us about his journey of recovery from addiction and compulsions that kept him from living the abundant life that Jesus has in mind for us. All of us can identify with his struggles. Hopefully some of us can also learn from his many practical suggestions and insights."

—**Reggie McNeal,** author, *A Work of Heart,* Missional Leadership
Specialist, Leadership Network

"Josh Reich's book *Breathing Room* is truly a breath of fresh air. You will appreciate Josh's authenticity and vulnerability as he shares his personal journey to try to find breathing room in his own life. This is the kind of book that is hard to pick up because you know you are going to be challenged to make life-altering changes; but it will be hard to put down because you know those changes are going lead you to discovering the abundant life that Jesus desires for all of us."

—**Brian Bloye,** senior pastor, West Ridge Church, co-author, *It's Personal*

BREATHING ROOM

BREATHING ROOM

Stressing Less & Living More

JOSH REICH

LEAFWOOD
PUBLISHERS
an imprint of Abilene Christian University Press

BREATHING ROOM
Stressing Less & Living More

LEAFWOOD
P U B L I S H E R S
an imprint of Abilene Christian University Press

Published in association with The Blythe Daniel Agency, Inc., PO Box 64197, Colorado Springs, CO 80962.

Cover design by Thinkpen Design, LLC
Interior text design by Sandy Armstrong, Strong Design

Leafwood Publishers is an imprint of
Abilene Christian University Press
ACU Box 29138
Abilene, Texas 79699

1-877-816-4455
www.leafwoodpublishers.com

15 16 17 18 19 20 / 7 6 5 4 3 2 1

To Katie,
for walking with me on the journey to breathing room.
Life really is better with breathing room.

Acknowledgments

A book like this doesn't come together with just one person. My journey to breathing room has been filled with people all along the way who have not only made the choice to have breathing room with me, but also challenge me to create space in my life.

The elders, staff, and people of Revolution Church have decided to live in a simple, intentional way so that we can experience all that God has for us. They have not only allowed me the space to experiment to find the solutions in this book, but they also created the space for me to write it. Encouraging me and praying for me all along the way. They also continually challenge me to not slip back into an unsustainable pace.

My agent, Blythe, believed in me and this book when no one else did. You saw a book in me and encouraged me, challenged me, and helped focus this book into what it is. It is hard to believe that this whole process started almost four years ago.

My wife, Katie, walked with me through some incredibly dark moments (which make up a lot of this book). We walked together to the other side, and we are stronger for it. I still remember sitting with you and wondering if we could find breathing room, or if it was a mirage taunting us. It is real. It is worth fighting for; and I'm grateful you stuck it out and believed it was possible.

Contents

Chapter 1

Close Quarters

I had no clue that on a normal date night everything in my life was headed toward change, that I was about to learn what it feels like to suffocate, to find myself trapped in tight emotional quarters, desperate for some breathing room.

This date with my wife, Katie, started like so many others. The kids were safe at home with the sitter, and we were driving to the movie theater, feeling like we were dating again, only without kids. It was a total feeling of relief to be on our way. You know what it's like when someone high-fives you—a "go for it" type of moment! This was a special occasion, because Katie thinks paying to see a movie in a theater—while also having to hire a babysitter—is a waste of money. She has a point, but I really like the big screen, so I was excited that we were in the car and on our way.

When it comes to choosing a movie at our house, Katie rarely has a strong preference. Thankfully, she and I like the same kind of movies, so we don't ever have that fight. On the way to the theater, I was telling her the options and she gave me her standard line: "I don't have an opinion; just pick one."

Now, this may be just a little strange, but when I was a kid I didn't dream about being a fireman when I grew up—I wanted to be a movie critic! I liked movies so much that the idea of getting paid to watch them seemed like something out of a fantasy world. So, to this day, I always have a list of movies I want to see.

This night was no different. I had two in mind that I thought would be perfect—*Tinker Tailor Soldier Spy* and *Sherlock Holmes: A Game of Shadows*—except I couldn't decide which one to choose. They started at the same time, were about the same length, and had equally good reviews. The drive to the theater took twenty minutes, and the entire way I waffled on my decision. Katie tried to help, but I couldn't make up my mind.

We pulled into the theater lot and walked to the ticket line. I was still unsure, rapidly flopping back and forth between the two pictures. I stared at the movies listed above the ticket counter, hoping for some burst of inspiration. Finally it was our turn, and in a near panic, I bought the tickets to *Tinker Tailor Soldier Spy*. And, almost immediately, I had buyer's remorse, but now I was stuck! With the tickets in hand, we bought popcorn and found our seats.

We were early, so we were treated to all the ads and short previews showing before the actual movie previews. This just gave me more time to rethink—and regret—my choice, and now, for no good reason, I was getting angry. It made me mad that I had chosen *this* movie, which seemed vastly inferior to the other one.

I know this sounds crazy—but hang in here with me. I'm sure I'm not the only one who has ever felt so torn about something so minor that had the power to affect me so greatly.

So while the pre-previews were still rolling, I leaned close to Katie and asked, "Can we go to the other movie?" She's awesome—she didn't even roll her eyes, just smiled and said that was fine with her.

Now, if you knew me personally, you would agree that this flip-flopping behavior was not characteristic. I am normally a decisive person, and I will fight to the death for an idea I believe in. I set goals and accomplish them. But on this night I was wavering, unsure.

Sherlock Holmes: A Game of Shadows was showing in the theater next door, so in a couple of minutes we had moved and were settled in our seats.

I seemed settled and all ready to go.

It happened again.

I kid you not—in the next ten minutes we must have switched theaters five times! Katie was incredibly gracious the entire time, patiently following me back and forth as we traded theaters.

Finally, we stopped playing "musical theaters," not because I was certain about which movie to watch, but because the previews had started. I'm such a movie freak that I think if you miss any of the previews, it's not worth watching the movie!

As *Sherlock Holmes: A Game of Shadows* started, I was able to relax a little, but something happened about thirty-five minutes into the movie that alarmed me. Again I started getting angry—not "stand up and start throwing things" angry, but seriously annoyed. I leaned over to Katie and whispered, "I can't believe we picked this movie!" Notice I said *we*—how unfair to my tolerant wife! "We should've gone to the other movie."

Right there in the movie theater, I kicked off a pity party because we were seeing the movie I had chosen! And on top of it, I wanted Katie to take some of the "blame." All she said was, "We're not switching theaters again." (I love my wife!)

The movie ended, and still stuck in my self-imposed funk, I slouched out of the theater. I had just spent our hard-earned money on two hours of fuming. When we got into the car, Katie looked at me and asked, "What is wrong? This is not like you. What is happening?"

I'm sure she braced herself for the worst, but all I could say was, "I have no idea." That was the truth. My mind was racing, trying to figure out why I couldn't make up my mind about a simple movie. And even more, I couldn't understand why I felt as if I was suffocating.

Chips, Salsa, and the Beginning of Breathing Room

We drove in silence to one of our favorite date-night eating spots, and as we ate chips and salsa, waiting to order, Katie asked me again, "What is wrong? This isn't like you."

For a long time I didn't answer and sat in a sad silence. Finally I opened the curtain slightly and let her peek at one thing I knew was troubling me. I told her I was miserable and no longer had a passion for my job. All the things I normally take joy in or find excitement in doing—or that are easy for me to do—I no longer wanted to do. In fact, the parts of my job that I love, like preaching and casting vision for my church, were now painful and arduous tasks.

Every time the phone rang or an email announced another meeting, my heart would sink as I calculated the cost in energy to do these tasks. And it wasn't just my job that made me feel like this. I was also having difficulty finding the strength and enthusiasm to play with our kids. Just getting out of bed in the morning seemed to be taking almost everything out of me. At the best of times, I woke up on a mission, set to tackle the day; but now I was the opposite.

I told Katie that between the services at church when I preached, I would hang out in a back room by myself so that I wouldn't have to talk to anybody. Even though I loved people, being around them was the last thing I wanted to do.

All the emotions I had held in check for a long time—over a year—flooded out, feelings of hurt, sadness about my life, worry about my depleted energy. For some time I'd felt my life had been an emotional roller coaster, and I wasn't sure where the ups and downs ended.

What I shared that night over the chips and salsa were things that no one knew—not Katie, close friends, my church staff, or the elders of my church. Nobody. I didn't use these words to describe how I felt then, but now I know: *I was out of breathing room.*

Sharing my heart with Katie was a huge step for me, because I had to admit I had a weakness. Like many people, I had built much of my identity on my strength—not physical strength but emotional muscle. I had encouraged others to think I had a bulletproof exterior that could stand up to anything. I had the mentality that I could outlast anyone emotionally or mentally. Admitting weakness was not a part of my game plan for life.

But this moment, prompted by my crazy indecision over the movie, was different. I was done. I felt weak and lost.

I didn't know what else to do.

As counterintuitive as it may seem, a moment of truth like this is crucial for our health, relationships, career, and ultimately our lives. It's the moment when you hear yourself say, "I can't keep doing life this way. I feel trapped and am having a hard time getting enough air to breathe." That moment when you look at your finances and say, "I'm done living beyond my means because it is making me miserable as I drown in debt."

Many miss this and continue pushing. "Breathing room," according to Andy Stanley, is "the space between your current pace and your limits."[1] At this moment, I had hit my limit.

Maybe you are there now. It might be your finances where you have hit your limit. You have been buying things, pushing debt payments into the future in hopes of something coming together, but your pace of spending is now at its limit. It might be your health. Your pace of sleep, work, and eating have now reached the limit of what your body can physically handle. It might be your schedule. The number of activities your kids do, the number of committees and teams you are on has now reached your limit.

Maybe it's time for you to say, "I'm out of breathing room," as I did.

The Important First Step

As I poured out to Katie what the last sixteen months of my life had been like, she mainly listened. She pressed for more information on certain comments, but mostly just listened.

She had noticed. While I had tried to conceal my stress, tried to push through it, she had noticed. She had tried to figure out how to help me, but I wouldn't let her in. She had tried to be a buffer between me and our kids, hoping that I would relax and not be too on edge around them and her. It wasn't a fear, she told me, more of just uneasiness as to what my mood would be like and how it would affect her and the kids. She had tried to tell me to sleep more, but I always had a reason why I wanted to stay up late or get up early. She had encouraged me to take a retreat day or slow down during the week, but I always had a reason why I couldn't.

Although it felt good to let the cork pop on my pent-up feelings, it didn't last long. I still felt terribly stuck.

As soon as I was done talking, I remembered that I had a job—I was expected to preach tomorrow! I had a growing family to help parent and decisions to make that affected other people. But I felt paralyzed . . . and, honestly, really didn't want to do anything!

So I took an important first step: I made a choice about my immediate future—specifically *tomorrow*. That act is crucial to finding breathing room: *I admitted I was gasping for air and sought help.*

That decision might seem like a no-brainer, but one of the reasons many people don't experience breathing room is the same reason I went so long without it: I never admitted to anybody that I needed help. And to myself that I needed more margin in areas of my life.

When I got home that night after my chips and salsa meltdown with Katie, I emailed the elders and told them I needed to talk with them after church the next day. They may have feared the worst after that message: *What does he want to talk about? Has he had a moral failure? Is he quitting?*

This is the scary moment—the moment when you and others realize that the game is changing. The fear of the unknown, in particular the fear about how those closest to you will react to your "news," is what keeps many people running at an exhausting pace. "I might lose my job," or "People will think I'm not capable of carrying it all" are common worries we have. The possible "what-if" fears are endless, but here are some common ones:

- How will my spouse respond to a change of schedule or budget?
- How will my kids fare if I keep them off the sports team next season?
- What will happen to my career track if I put in fewer hours at work?
- What will the leaders at church say if I can't lead a small group now?
- If I change my pace or budget, will I miss out on something?

This moment of fear can keep us from finding breathing room for several reasons: we fear losing control, missing out, falling behind, or having a life that won't *count* significantly.

The fear is real. But God's presence with us is also real. I needed to hold on to that promise then as I have countless times since.

The next day Katie and I met with the elders, and as I shared with them my struggle and how I was feeling, I entered into a deeper level of vulnerability. In the past I was the one who led most of these meetings. This time I was not in charge, and I walked into the meeting without knowing the outcome. I was literally at their mercy.

As I had done the night before with Katie, I sketched out how the pressures and stress of life had gotten to me in the past sixteen months. These elders were well aware of all the things that had happened in our growing church—many of them exciting breakthroughs in ministry. But they had also been challenging, exhausting times, which included a merger with another church and a four-month protracted interaction and conflict with a now-departed church leader. I also had had a health scare, which I realized later was a point where God tried to slow me down. Often it's not what happens *to* us but what happens *in* us that leads us to consider our pace and life. Thinking back to that as I spoke with the elders, I was reminded of just how close I had come to living a life completely devoid of the health that I so desperately wanted.

A Preacher with No Voice

It all had started on a Friday night. My sermon preparation was done, and after taking a run to unwind, I had come home to clean up. When I stepped out of the shower, I had no voice. Literally. When I opened my mouth, I could not talk. Nothing. No sound!

This was one of the scariest events of my life. I went to the doctor and he told me to take it easy and rest my voice for ten days. This was a very humbling circumstance for a man who does a lot of talking as part of his work! As I waited silently those days, all I could think of was, *What if my voice never comes back? What will I do for a job? How will I make money? What will happen to my family? Will we be homeless?*

Through this trial I had kept working, kept moving, kept busy in hopes that tomorrow my voice would be better. I've found that's what we tend to do when we are out of breathing room:

we try to find a quick fix for the problem, a change of scenery, or if all else fails, we keep doing—more frantically—what got us in trouble in the first place. We don't slow down much. We try to fill our time with *more* rather than *less*. And that takes us further and further from the breathing room we need.

Thankfully, after the ten days my voice did return, but the experience shook me. I saw how vulnerable we are to events outside our control. But after I felt better, I didn't really change anything that I was doing. And I have come back to that at times to ask myself, "You can get your voice back, but do you have the space in your life that you really need? Not just a voice to say more, explain more, and do more."

The Two Weeks That Changed My Life

When I finished unloading my story to the church leaders, Katie and I waited, having no idea what would happen next. The elders asked some questions, including one about whether or not I had a plan on how to move forward. I told them I did but that I wanted their input too.

We decided together that I would take the next two weeks off from preaching, read some books on topics related to the issues I was facing, and visit with my personal physician, who also treats adrenal fatigue and advises on overall wellness, to try to figure out what had happened to me and how I would recover.

What I learned over those two weeks, and the changes I've made since that moment, truly changed my life. I'm a living testimony that breathing room, which once seemed a fantasy to me, is possible! Living at a sustainable pace, dealing with the hurt in our lives, and moving past addictions that have ensnared us for years can happen. And the surreal freedom I felt once I acknowledged the problem and made big changes in my life is something I don't want to ever forget. And that's the purpose of this book. I don't want anyone else to experience the angst, fatigue, uncertainty, and cloudiness that I felt. If my story can help just one person, it's worth it to me to share my experiences with others who are going through a lack of breathing room.

The first two weeks after that night were a great beginning, but it took almost a year to unravel everything that had put me where I was and that had negatively affected those closest to me. That year was spent uncovering the past hurts, secret addictions, and pain that I had tried to shut out instead of living in the freedom Jesus has from them. That freedom is the freedom I hope for you to experience.

One of the reasons people are gasping for air today is that we expect *breathing room to be found instantly.* What we forget is that we typically have spent months or even years living at a certain pace, ignoring the feelings and hurt we carried around. Then we expect to get over it in a flash. We put too much pressure on ourselves, and then we're right back to no breathing room again.

As I write this, I'm sitting by a pool on vacation with my family in San Diego. The difference in me between that evening at the movie theater and today is astonishing. Was that agitated, burned-out, growing-cynical guy really me? Yes, it was—and I much prefer the new person I'm becoming, now that I have plenty of room to breathe!

Today, our church has a larger presence and growing number of people from our community, and my own family, through adoption, has increased from three to five kids. I'm healthier, both physically and emotionally. I look at both the world and myself differently. I no longer try to squeeze everything I can out of life, because when we try, life has a way of squeezing us. Instead, I try to live and experience life each moment, each day.

When you slow down, take a break, have a long conversation with a friend, take a nap, or skip a soccer season, you will miss some things. But what you will gain is a fuller experience of life. You will feel more alive because you have room to breathe. It's not always easy for me and Katie, and we have had to say no to a lot, which felt huge at the time. But we can honestly say that even though we have more responsibility now than we did then, we feel as if we have room in our lives to be able to take on our roles, friends, ministry, and family in a much healthier way. And that's something we are both grateful for.

Your Journey to Breathing Room

How about you—is your day-to-day life squeezing the air out of you? I want to encourage you at this point to take an inventory of your life—and the pace of your life. Your story may have put you in a very bad place. You may be searching for breathing room because of a heart attack or the loss of a spouse who decided to walk away. You may have missed opportunities with your kids because of the pace you've lived. Because of past hurts, you may have lost the joy of relationships because you are afraid to let anyone get close.

It's not too late. It's never too late! The exact place that seems so hopeless is where God can do the most. Finding room to breathe will take work, and it usually happens very intentionally over a period of time. But breathing room is possible for anyone, regardless of circumstances. The life Jesus came to give you (see John 10:10) is overflowing and abundant.

The material in this book is not a quick or magical fix. But once you decide to change how you respond to all the pressures you face, progress will begin and you, too, can experience a life that has space you can enjoy living in . . . *breathing room.*

The pages that follow are a road map of sorts. Think of this book as your own two-week experience—like the time my elders gave me to figure out how to move forward.

We'll start by looking at what causes life to close in—the relationships, choices, and commitments that make us gasp for breathing room and keep us from living as we were created to live. Then we'll figure out why those things crowd out our life. Finally we'll look at how we can make the changes that will allow us to bring much-needed fresh air deep into our lives.

Most of us know one of God's commandments to his people first given in the Old Testament, which is to take a day of rest. This intentional breathing room can be so hard for us, even for one day. Think about the last time you did this. Many of us don't know how to breathe on our own for one day, much less at a sustainable rate throughout the week, so we'll spend some time talking about this.

Breathing New Air

At the end of each chapter there will be a section called *Breathing New Air*. It is a space to journal, answer questions, and think about what is covered in each chapter.

As we begin our journey together, the first step you need to take toward breathing new air is to turn the page and begin looking at what is keeping you from *breathing room.*

Discussion Questions

1. How can you relate to Josh's story?

2. Read Matthew 11:28–30.

3. What things are weighing you down right now? List them.

4. What would it look like to give them to Jesus and take his yoke (which is light) on your shoulders?

5. Describe how your life would be different if you lived these verses.

6. What fears do you have about making changes to your life to have breathing room?

Chapter 2

The Balancing Act of Life

I don't know if every family has balance as a goal, but I believe all families want a more sustainable life. They long for life to be slower, more stable or controllable. Yet no matter what they do, they always feel as though they are running from one thing to the next, always participating in the next sport, the next class, the next committee. Their to-do list grows at an incredible rate, and while all this happens, they see their stress level increase, their sleep decrease, and they feel like they are missing out.

Yet they still go for the elusive goal of balance.

But what is balance? How do you know if you have reached that goal?

If you were to ask your friends, what would they say? I have begun asking people, "How do you know if you are balancing work and home life well?"

One of the great mysteries in our culture is that everyone is reaching for a goal of balancing life, but no one is sure what that looks like—only that they should be going for it.

Your Typical Day

Your alarm goes off at 6 A.M. The morning is often a fight to get out of bed. Not just for you, but also for your kids. In the kitchen, it is every man for himself if Mom hasn't been able to make breakfast or the kids don't like what you have prepared. Still, sometimes you eat breakfast, sometimes you don't. It all depends on how much time you have and how much you're needed to help with the kids.

By 6:45, you are out the door in hopes of beating the traffic. Mom and the kids are usually out the door by 7:15. After dropping off the kids at school, she either spends twenty minutes driving to work or begins a day of errands, meetings, and following up from the day before.

From the moment you step into your office, it is one thing after another. By the time you finish writing one email to put out a fire, another one flies across your computer, creating two new fires, and the email you just sent is now obsolete. Every meeting ends with more things on your to-do list, and you walk back to your office dreading how many phone calls and emails you missed while in that meeting. Each meeting you attend seems to result in more meetings.

Lunch is at your desk, just trying to catch up. Because you rushed out the door, you forgot to pack a lunch, so you eat whatever you can find around the office or make a quick run to McDonald's. You know you shouldn't eat it, but it is fast and cheap. You get the large soda in hopes of the caffeine kicking in and helping you make it through the afternoon.

Finally that dreaded moment hits: 2 P.M. The afternoon lull. You remember the commercial you saw for 5-hour ENERGY the night before and wonder if that would help. You've already had four cups of coffee, a large soda, a Big Mac, large fries, and half a donut. You just need to survive three more hours. Your health and energy level pay the real price each day.

When the kids are out of school at 3:30, it is a rush to get them. One child spends a couple of hours in an after-school program, and one parent will leave work early to get the child and arrive home before 5:30.

Now this is when it gets interesting. One child has a baseball game at 6:15 and another has one at 6:30. Both games are at different fields. After the time spent picking up the kids and the rush of getting home and changing clothes, dinner will have to wait. So will homework; there's no time before the game.

When you finally get to the field, you can take a quick minute to catch your breath. As you watch your son play, you begin to think through your day. You wonder what, if anything, you accomplished. You try not to think about tomorrow, and you want to forget about work, but it is all you can think about.

While you're sitting there, you figure you can knock out some work. Why not? You are thinking about work, so you might as well work. So you pull out your phone and start going through emails. It always amazes you how many emails you can get in a day. Then your phone rings. It is Bruce from the office. He wants to know if you got his email. You tell him, "I'm at my son's baseball game, but I'm looking through my email now." He wants to know what you think about his idea.

The conversation takes twenty minutes, and the game is over by that time. Your thoughts drift toward how you are running from one thing to the next without taking time to really be present with your son. *Is this the life that God intended? How does this affect my relationships with my kids?* you wonder. Surely there must be a point at which the "extras" in your schedule level out?

It is now 8 P.M. By the time you get home, it's later, and no one has thought about dinner. You scour the fridge and realize there isn't really anything to eat. *Doesn't anybody do any grocery shopping in this family?* you wonder. You call your wife. She is on her way home, so she grabs some takeout for everybody.

By the time she gets home, it is 8:30. Your son is in the living room playing his Xbox. When you finally get his attention, he tells you he isn't hungry and that he has a big project due tomorrow, which no one else knew anything about until that moment.

You hit the roof because you know that this will now take up what is left of your evening, and any hope of relaxing has just gone out the window.

At the end of the day, you've run all over town, have a to-do list that will take a month to complete, and by the time you and your wife roll into bed at 11 P.M. you are too tired to sleep. Your mind is racing with all the things you need to do.

You try to relax by turning on the TV and watching it while lying in bed. You want to ask your wife about sex, but she is already asleep and you know how that goes. You feel like your relationship with your wife is suffering because of the schedules you keep. The pace at which you both work and live has affected your relationship not only physically but spiritually. There was a time when you prayed together, talked through your day, and felt connected to each other, but those feel like distant memories.

By the time you finally turn off the TV and look at the clock, you see the red numbers display 12:15. You sigh, knowing that tomorrow will be another long day.

This Is Normal

If your days look anything like this, you are probably thinking about how long you can keep this up. Maybe you felt stress or your heart raced just from reading it. Breathing room? No one has time for breathing room—not when you run from one thing to the next.

For most Americans, this is life. We pay for this life. But this is the dream we all grow up wanting, don't we? Running from one activity to the next, feeling exhausted and run-down every night.

How often is your week simply a rush to get to the weekend? Then the weekend arrives, and before you know it, it is over. You walk into work on Monday morning and you think, "What happened to my weekend?"

Vacations can be the same. After one vacation I was asked by close to ten people, "Now that you are back from your vacation, do you need a vacation from your vacation?"

In fact, it is no longer abnormal to be tired, burned out, stressed, or haggard. It is normal. Our kids feel it too. I once talked with a family at our church whose four-year-old daughter was being treated for a stress-related disease. When I asked if they knew what caused it or if they would make any changes to their lives, the mom just shrugged, as if this was as normal as a child catching a cold.

Fatigue

So how do you know if you are fatigued, on the verge of burning out?

Here are some indicators:

- Your reaction to situations does not match the situation. You get angry at small things or cry without knowing why.
- You struggle to make simple decisions and find yourself paralyzed at making a choice (as I described in Chapter One).
- You have impulses to eat and drink, and you struggle to control them.
- You think short term instead of long term.
- You have less courage.
- You are more irritable.

My Life

My life is a lot like your life in this regard. I am the father of five kids. I pastor a growing church that my wife and I started with a group of twelve people. I do leadership coaching for other church planters, speak to groups, and preach every week at my church. My kids are in art club, sports teams, gymnastics, and horse lessons. We have school each day. We are part of a small group at our church, so we have people in our home at least twice a week. Between working fifty hours a week, trying to work out regularly, keeping the flame of my marriage alive and well, and spending time with my kids, it can get busy, and sometimes overwhelming with all of our responsibilities.

Before you get the idea that what I'm about to share with you is easy, you should know that none of this is easy. The journey in this area of pacing ourselves and finding breathing room has been hard for our family. It takes courage and unlearning a lot of old patterns.

To live at a sustainable pace will mean that you will miss out on some things. If you look at your life right now and would say it is *not* a sustainable pace, you need to know that some things will need to change for your life to become sustainable.

When we started Revolution Church in 2008, like most church planters we jumped headlong into building our church. There were eighty-hour work weeks and little sleep. In the first two years of Revolution, I preached almost a hundred times. During this time, I tried to exercise to manage part of my stress, but it was hard. Between late nights, lunch meetings, and small kids at home, it never seemed to get easier.

As I shared in Chapter One, I hit a wall physically and emotionally in 2011. I was burned out, with no breathing room to speak of. According to Dr. James Wilson, author of *Adrenal Fatigue: The 21st Century Stress Syndrome,* medical professionals, teachers, and pastors are the most likely to suffer from adrenal fatigue, and I fell into this category of allowing my schedule to railroad my body, so to speak.

It was an incredibly hard year for Katie and me, and we didn't handle it well. The church was growing. During this year we had two elders leave our team: one who started a new ministry and the other under really difficult circumstances involving sin. The problem for me was that I never fully dealt with the impacts of these situations.

Interestingly, burnout doesn't always just come from working too much. While burning the candle at both ends will eventually leave you in the dark with no candle (and burned out), not dealing with the emotional roller coaster of life will also lead you there.

Balance Is a Pipe Dream

The first thing I learned in the two weeks off that my elders gave me had to do with goals we have for our lives and how we spend our time. I talked with a number of people during that time and shared my plight with them. The answers were almost always the same: "You need to have more balance in your life." When I would ask what that looks like, I would get silence and blank stares.

We want balance because our lives feel out of balance and we hear others say that balance is the goal. While this is the goal for most people, no one seems to know what it looks like, feels like, or if it is even possible.

I began to realize that balance is a pipe dream. In fact, you won't find the idea of balancing your life anywhere in Scripture. Instead, it seems as if Jesus goes to extremes. He calls people to leave everything to follow him, to die to themselves, and pick up their crosses. That doesn't sound like balance.

We are also told that God created a rhythm for us of work and rest. We are to work six days and rest one. This is one significant way that we reflect how God created us to live. Because we are constantly connected to work through our emails and smartphones, the problem for most Americans is not that they rest too much;

it is that they work too much and don't rest enough. We lack breathing room, even though, from the beginning of the Bible, God commanded us to have breathing room.

Think about how connected you are right now. We check email during dinner, jump every time our phone beeps, and struggle not to check Facebook or email on vacation or during the weekend. Often we're afraid we will miss something, or we think we are indispensable. Yet the long-term effect of our connectivity is becoming more and more clear. We don't pace ourselves, nor do we live at a sustainable pace.

The reality of disconnecting electronically is difficult. Try it for a night. Turn your phone off. No calls, texts, emails, or social media. You will go through withdrawal much like an addict does.

For better or worse, the consumption of media, as varied as email and TV, has exploded. We live in the excess of it. Computer users at work change windows or check email nearly 37 times an hour, research shows.

More than likely, this isn't news to you. You are reading this book because you live this struggle. This is your daily plight.

Why We Don't Rest

Not many of us think about any consequences if we do not shut down for a day of rest—mainly we fear a missed email or opportunity. In Scripture, there are numerous verses on rest. In Exodus 20, God commands his people to work six days and rest one. In Matthew 11, Jesus tells his followers that we are to take his yoke and give him our burdens, to let go of things. Psalm 46 tells us that we are to be still and know that we are not God.

These verses feel impossible to live in our culture. The average American worker has fourteen days of vacation a year and takes twelve.

Worse than that, about 25% of Americans don't take any vacation days at all. The U.S. is the only industrialized nation in the world that does not legally require workers to be provided a set number of paid vacation days. This is in stark contrast to Europe where the European Union mandates that workers be provided with 20 paid vacation days every year. Do you want to guess which has higher life expectancy? European countries win, of course. In fact, the U.S. is 28th in the world in life expectancy.[1]

So why don't we rest? I think there are three simple reasons:

- We have to admit we aren't God.
- We have to stop.
- We have to know God, not just know about God.

Let's take the first one; we have to admit we aren't God. This is difficult for many of us. We live as if our office or our home would fall apart if we took a day off. We feel that powerful and in control. This belief is what keeps many of us running faster and faster. We have to admit there are things outside of our control—things we can't handle. Whenever we rest, we are affirming that God is in control and we are not.

The second reason is that we don't like to stop. The reason many of us are doing more and more and staying as busy as we can isn't because we would be bored otherwise (although many think they will be bored if they slow down). We don't like silence. When we stop, we run the risk of being able to feel things from our past, including the hurts and memories we have carried for years. We'll look more at handling our past later in the book, but have you ever realized that you might be exhausted and busy so that you don't have to deal with past hurts, the issues in your marriage, or your lack of community?

The third reason is that we don't *really* know God. Psalm 46 tells us to "know God," and this knowledge will lead us to be still. Because when we know God, his grace and his mercy will cause us to be still. As long as we live as if we don't really know God, we can't rest in the truths of how he has made us to live: with breathing room and with more margin than we're allowing ourselves. Until then, these boundaries may seem, at best, pretty good ideas.

Yes and No

So how do we alter our life patterns that clearly aren't working? There is an incredibly simple time-management principle that has guided my decisions and how I manage my time that I believe is a game changer. While it is simple, it has far-reaching implications. Here it is:

Every time you say *yes* to something, you say *no* to something else.

If you run a company or a church, you can't do everything. In your family, you can't afford everything; you can't sign up your child for every activity (although lots of parents try).

It's very simple. If you say yes to something, you will have to say no to something else. I was talking with a couple recently, and they were wrestling with whether or not the wife should go back to work. They have small kids, money is tight, and they said, "It would help us financially." I told them this premise and said, "If you say yes to working, you will make money. But you will be spending less time with your kids while someone else takes charge of raising them, and you will be bringing stress into your life that isn't there now because you will be home less."

Every day we make choices about how to spend our time. When a man chooses between spending time on the golf course or at the lake with his buddies versus spending time with his children, he is saying yes to something and no to something else. We might say yes to what we want to do, but at the same time say no to investing in our kids or an important relationship.

At the end of the workday, if we say yes to working late, we are saying no to a sustainable pace, no to spending time with family or friends who could help us unwind.

Pastors struggle with this in their churches as many churches pack their church calendars with more and more programs and activities. "If we have a program for everybody, we will reach everybody," the thinking goes. But if you shoot to reach everybody, you will reach nobody. You can't say yes to every kind of music, dress, style, and service time. Pick one.

As a pastor, there are many people to meet with. You don't want to say no to anyone because they might leave, and you need everyone you can get—all the givers you can muster up, especially when you are a newly planted church. This often leads to you running yourself ragged, not resting well, and not spending time with your family or with Jesus. We rationalize that we're serving people, helping them, and that next month we'll take that Sabbath or that date night.

As a parent, it is easy to do this as we run our kids from one activity to the next in an effort to give them a well-rounded life. By doing that—by saying yes to running our kids everywhere—we are saying no to family dinners and often to family devotions, and we are saying yes to more stress in life. Many couples sacrifice their marriages for their kids, pouring their time and energy into their kids instead of their marriage, making their relationship with their kids the most important relationship in the family. This is one reason why more divorces happen in year twenty-five of married life than any other year. Empty nesters don't know each other without their kids.

In our family, we say yes to exercising and a healthy lifestyle. Every time we go to the gym or make a meal plan to eat a healthy diet, we are saying yes to health and longevity in life. I have to say no to sleeping in (so I can get to the gym by 6 A.M.), to late-night snacks, to too many chicken wings, and to swearing off my beloved White Chocolate Mocha Frappuccino (I feel like I just gained a pound by typing the words).

When we got married, we decided I would work and Katie would stay home. We said yes to her staying home and no to a lot of other things. Other families have nicer things or go on nicer vacations than we do because of this choice. That's okay. When we made this choice, we knew what we were saying yes and no to.

We say yes to spending time with certain people and no to others. Many people feel the strain of wanting to be with people and spending time with as many people as possible. But it is simply impossible. You can't have a relationship with everyone you want a relationship with; you have to say yes to some and no to others.

When someone asks if they can meet with me or a friend wants to hang out, I want to help them and say yes. Often I'm able to, but many times if I say yes to that opportunity, I will have to say no to something else. It might be a date night with Katie, time with my kids, a nap that I need, or my sermon prep time. When we say yes to the wrong things, it is often because we want to make someone approve of us or be comfortable in a relationship.

It feels harsh to say no to people. Andy Stanley in his book *Deep and Wide* shares that all of us couldn't do everything for everybody no matter how much we'd like to be able to. We can't meet everyone's needs or be at everything. There just isn't enough time in the day or energy in our bodies to do it. So we should *do for one what we'd like to do for everyone*. You can't help everyone financially or help everyone move, but you can do something for someone.

Pace and Your Body

We talked about the concept of rhythm earlier. People who live in rhythm, who rest and recharge well, are not only healthier, but they are more productive. A 2010 study found that 35 percent of Americans feel better about their jobs and are more productive after a vacation. Vacations have been found to help us recharge—we sleep better during them and for a period of time afterward. A common misperception we have is that if we work more hours, we are more productive. More and more evidence shows this isn't true. According to the same study in 2010,

> Greeks work the most in Europe—averaging 2,017 hours per year. Yet, they are no better off, as their

economy is a wreck. Now take a look at Germany—
Europe's economic powerhouse. You may guess that
the Germans work longer hours. Wrong. Germans work
on average 1,408 hours per year, placing them second
to last among the twenty-five European nations in
hours worked annually. They also receive on average
thirty paid vacation days a year—the most in Europe.[2]

It doesn't take a rocket scientist to know that people who work less, take their vacation days, and honor the Sabbath live healthier, happier lives. The problem for many of us is that we don't know where to start. In fact, it can feel paralyzing.

Sabbath in the Midst of a Connected Life

Sabbath may be a foreign concept to you. Maybe like me, you have spent much of your life seeking balance. You aren't sure what balance looks like, but that's what people told you to find. You aren't sure your friends have balance, but they at least seem less tired than you.

Let's start at the end of our day, which is the beginning of the day in Scripture: going to sleep. If you read Genesis 1, as God is creating all things, it says, "There was evening, and there was morning." Scripture starts at sundown. The Sabbath for the people of God starts at sundown. We need this mindset as we think about our days and as we move toward breathing room in our schedules.

In our culture, though, we start our days in the morning. So when we talk about how to start our day right, we think strictly about our morning routine and getting out of bed.

What if this is why it is backward for us and we struggle with breathing room?

When was the last time you thought about how your day ended and how that affected the coming day?

It's no secret that one of the reasons many Americans lack breathing room in their lives is because of a lack of sleep. One of the most common complaints I hear from people about stress or a lack of breathing in life stems from a lack of sleep, so let's start there.

How do you get a good night's sleep?

Here are a few ideas:

1. *Wake up when your alarm goes off.* We love hitting the snooze button, feeling like we are getting extra sleep, but when we do this, we feel more tired.

2. *Don't eat late.* When you are in college, eating a pizza at midnight is just part of the landscape, but now that you are older, try to stop eating by 8 P.M. If you can have dinner by 6:30, even better.

3. *Be in bed by 10 P.M.* This was the hardest one for me to do. I love staying up late and would watch TV well past midnight, but that left me incredibly groggy and tired in the morning. My wife would go to bed at 8 P.M. if I let her, so she helped me with this. If you think this sounds crazy (as I did), start by going to bed thirty minutes earlier and keep working toward 10 P.M. I've noticed that my body begins to get tired before 10 now, and if I don't go to bed, I start to wake up more (this is called a second wind), and that keeps me from getting a good night's sleep.

4. *No caffeine in the afternoon.* Sometimes drinking coffee in the afternoon is okay; but for the most part, the less caffeine, chocolate, or black tea you consume in the afternoon or evening, the better.

5. *Quiet yourself before bed.* Don't watch an action movie or a sporting event and then try to go to sleep. Do something that doesn't stress you out or cause you to think about work. When you lie down, if you can't stop thinking, meditation and prayer can help to calm your mind.[3]

What happens to us if we don't heed this advice on sleep? Honestly? There are a lot of consequences to us not sleeping well and not getting adequate sleep. Here are some from a list compiled by David Murray (I realize the list is long, but I want us to understand the consequences if we neglect sleep):

- Just one week of sleeping fewer than six hours a night results in changes to more than 700 genes.
- Just one night of sleep deprivation is linked with signs of brain tissue loss.
- Infection-fighting antibodies and cells are reduced during periods when we don't get enough sleep.
- Sleeping fewer than seven hours a night is associated with a *tripled* risk of coming down with a cold.
- Sleep loss increases hunger, portion size, and preference for high-calorie, high-carb foods, with the resulting risk of obesity.
- Chronic sleep deprivation (less than 6 hours a night) is associated with: Skin aging, 4 x stroke risk for middle- and older-aged people, 50% higher risk of colorectal

cancers, and some links with other cancers too, High blood pressure, 48% higher chance of developing or dying from heart disease and lower fertility rates.

- Sleep flushes dangerous proteins from your brain, improving mental health. "When you're sleep deprived, you get a dirty brain."
- Sleep allows the brain to consolidate and store the day's memories.
- Being exhausted zaps your focus, and can render you more forgetful.
- Chronic sleep deprivation in adolescents diminishes the brain's ability to learn new information.
- Sleep loss produces apathy, irritability, weepiness, impatience, anger, flattened responses.
- Sleep loss can cause psychological damage because sleep regulates the brain's flow of epinephrine, dopamine, and serotonin, chemicals closely associated with mood and behavior.
- People with insomnia are 10x as likely to develop depression and 17x as likely to have significant anxiety.
- The lack of sleep affects the teenage brain in similar ways to the adult brain, only more so, and can lead to emotional issues like depression and aggression.
- In one study by researchers at Columbia University, teens who went to bed at 10 P.M. or earlier were less likely to suffer from depression or suicidal thoughts than those who regularly stayed awake well after midnight.
- Undermines creativity, problem-solving ability, and productivity.

- Estimated to cost American businesses $63 billion a year.
- The worst costs arise from the fact that sleep deprivation causes safety lapses and contributes to other health issues.
- Other people (customers/clients) are likely to register a sleep-deprived person as lacking energy and unhealthy.
- 32 billion dollars a year spent on meds, mattresses, candles, sleep consultants, etc.
- 60 percent of grade school and high school children report that they are tired during the daytime and 15 percent of them admitted to falling asleep in class.
- Sleep deprivation is such a serious disruption that lessons have to be pitched at a lower level to accommodate sleep-starved learners.
- The United States has the highest number of sleep-deprived students, with 73% of 9- and 10-year-olds and 80% of 13- and 14-year-olds identified by their teachers as being adversely affected.
- In literacy tests, 76% of 9- and 10-year-olds were lacking sleep.
- Children who have more sleep achieve higher in maths, science and reading.
- A lack of sleep robs the fuel for self-control from the region of the brain responsible for self-control, whereas sleep restores it.
- Studies found that a lack of sleep led to high levels of unethical behavior.

- In tests, there was a difference of only about 22 minutes of sleep between those who cheated and those who did not.
- A lack of sleep leads to deviant behavior at work (like falsifying receipts), similarly because of decrements in self-control.[4]

Whether we want to admit it or not, the way we play with our sleep has drastic consequences for our social, emotional, financial, and spiritual well-being.

More than likely, though, this isn't a surprise to you. This is why we feel guilty as we watch a late-night show or eat ice cream at 11 P.M. It isn't that we don't know sleep is good for us; we struggle to know what resting looks like and why it is so good.

According to Mark Buchanan, author of *The Rest of God*, "Sabbath is both a day and an attitude to nurture stillness. It is both time on a calendar and a disposition of the heart. Sabbath imparts the rest of God—actual physical, mental, spiritual rest, but also the *rest* of God—the things of God's nature and presence we miss in our busyness."[5]

I grew up in a very legalistic church where you did absolutely nothing on Sunday. No movies, no shopping, no playing of games. People took a nap and sat around. That's probably not accurate, but as a five-year-old, that's the way it seemed. For many, this is our picture of Sabbath. Or, we wonder, "That sounds nice, but when do I have the time to stop?"

Recently I was talking with a couple who just got married. They were both in grad school and they were heavily involved at my church. They were lamenting their lack of time to rest and take the

Sabbath. They knew it was important and something they should do, but couldn't see how to make it work with everything else they were committed to. Notice that last line. One of the reasons we don't rest is we aren't sure how to make it happen within the confines of our calendar.

This is where the proverbial rubber meets the road.

Rest will require hard choices. I'm sure you are picking this up by now, but a sustainable pace, a life you want to live—resting, sleeping well, having community—will not just happen. Very few people that you know have those things going for them right now. It isn't because of lack of desire or lack of knowledge; it comes from our unwillingness to make the hard choices, our unwillingness to choose the short-term pain for the long-term gain.

As we talked, I shared a few things with them that I believe about resting well. Sabbath needs to be a full day. We give ourselves an out by saying, "I'll rest four hours here and four hours there." Our bodies need a sustained rest. God did not call us in Exodus 20 to take a morning off, but a day. He also didn't tell us what day it had to be. You need to figure out when resting makes sense in your schedule. For me, Sunday is a workday, so we pull back from our regular rhythm to rest on Monday. For you, it might be Tuesday. It might change as your kids get older or you become empty nesters.

Rest gets difficult when we realize that the reason we aren't resting is that we aren't willing to miss things. But people who live the life you and I are called to live, the life we were created to live, miss things. Their kids don't play on every sports team, they don't spend every evening at the baseball field, and they don't take all kinds of trips and go into all kinds of debt. They miss out on some of the things everyone else shoots for. Yet they enjoy a low stress level that few people experience. They have a full life that few people ever touch.

I'll often tell people something, and you will probably give me the reaction that I always get. But I'll tell you anyway, let you argue with me in your mind, and then explain why it is true.

Ready?

Here goes.

You have all the time you need to do everything you want to do.

Let me say that again.

You have all the time you need to do everything you want to do.

Another way of thinking about that is, everything that is important in your life happens.

I know what you are thinking. *My to-do list is a mile long. There are books I want to read, podcasts I want to listen to, TV shows I want to watch, friends I want to see more of, things I want to fix in my house or on my car, or a degree I'd like to finish.* If we were together right now, you would tell me I'm crazy.

Here's an example from my life: I'm an enormous Pittsburgh Steelers fan. When their schedule comes out every April, I immediately put all their games on my calendar. I get the NFL Sunday ticket so I don't miss any of their games. Do you know what happens? I don't miss any of their games. Why? It's important enough to get on my calendar.

The things that matter in our lives are assigned a minute. An hour. A time.

Very few things in your life happen accidentally. You don't accidentally fix the car. You don't accidentally work on your yard.

You don't accidentally take a camping trip with your kids or a date night with your spouse. You don't just happen to read your Bible. And you don't just happen to find yourself at the soccer field all weekend for a tournament. All those things happen because you give them a time and a place on your calendar.

The Guilt Involved

Let's talk about one other reason few people in our culture rest, and it is a reason very few people in the church talk about: guilt.

What I'm asking you to do could create a tinge of guilt in your mind. You want breathing room, you want to slow down and have a sustainable rhythm to your life, but you aren't sure where to start or if you want to make the changes for it to happen. The difficulty with breathing room when it comes to our schedules is how we compare ourselves to others. We think everyone around us has breathing room and is not as tired as we are. That's a lie.

While people, tasks, and situations bleed you dry of energy and life, you still can't imagine walking away from them. You can't imagine possibly ending that relationship. I understand. I've sat with countless people and counseled them through this, only to get to the end and hear them say, "But if I stop spending time with this person, it will hurt them." Yet they are simply dying inside every time they think of the person or the energy that relationship takes. We wonder how our kids will react to fewer activities, what our friends will think if we drop out of that committee at church, or how we'll be viewed at work if we turn down a promotion that means more time at work when we want more time with our kids.

Remember: *Those with breathing room choose their long-term happiness over short-term pain every time.*[6]

The Beginning of Breathing Room

As Katie and I began to take charge of our lives and find breathing room in our schedules by seeking rhythm, we started to realize something that is difficult to admit if you fill your life with people, places, and activities. Not everyone or everything is life-giving. Not everyone or everything is worth the same amount of time.

One of the things we did was sit down and make a list of the people, tasks, activities, and situations that rob us of energy or give us energy.

Take a minute. Put this book down, as long as you promise to come back to it. Pull out a piece of paper; draw a line down the center. At the top of one column write "Give energy," and at the top of the other column write "Rob energy." Now put every relationship, activity, task at home, work, or church you can think of in a column.

When Katie and I made our lists for people, tasks, and situations that rob us of energy or give us energy, we realized a few things. We were spending a lot of time with people who robbed us of energy. We had filled our calendar with things that were not life-giving, but that we felt we should do, things people expected us to do. In short, we did a lot of things that didn't fill us up and make us excited.

We also learned that we didn't know what was life-giving. Think about it. If you had an entire day with nothing on the schedule—a time when you could do anything you wanted and money wasn't an object, and at the end of the day you would feel filled up, rested, and recharged—most of us wouldn't know where to start. This is an exercise that we have come back to on a regular basis now and will continue to do as our kids get older and our stage of life changes.

As we looked at our lists, we realized we had to stop spending time with certain people. Some of those people didn't understand why we had to spend less time with them. The reality was that they sucked us dry of energy, and it was work to be with them. We took the short-term pain of having that conversation for long-term health.

I had to have a conversation with my elders (who are my bosses) and talk with them about tasks and situations that robbed me of energy. This conversation could've gone either way. After spending a few weeks praying about it and asking God to open their hearts, I shared with them things that were part of my job that I wanted to stop doing so that I could do other things. They were agreeable after I showed them that I wasn't simply trying to be lazy and pass off work "I didn't like to do."

I'm not suggesting that you call up everyone who robs you of energy and say, "I'm never talking to you again." Or talk to your boss and say, "I don't like doing these things, so I'm not doing them anymore."

Maybe for you it's housework, and to bring less stress in your life, you need to make a change in your budget and pay someone to clean your house. Maybe you spend five nights a week at the baseball field for your eight-year-old son, and it's now time to stop that so you can focus on him and your relationship *with* him.

Mark Buchanan writes, "The Sabbath golden rule is *Cease from what is necessary. Embrace that which gives life.*"[7] It is an opportunity for us to trust God and for God to give us rest.

So what is necessary for you to do on your next day off? Don't do it. What gives you life? Do that. I get life from having dinner with Katie and a couple of close friends, playing with my kids, watching the Steelers play, exercising, taking a hike in nature, reading a good book, or taking a nap. Those are things I strive to do on the day that I rest. For you, it might be gardening, working on your car, talking to an old friend, or just sitting quietly on your back porch.

If you want to have breathing room ten years from now, you have to make choices for breathing room *now*. It doesn't just happen.

Breathing New Air

As you look at your list of people, tasks, and situations that rob you of energy or give you energy, begin making changes to your schedule to spend more time with the energy givers, doing things that give you energy. Stop doing things that rob you of energy. This may take a couple of months to get used to, but start working toward it.

Look at your schedule. What things are you doing and what things did you say no to because of that choice? Are you okay with that? If not, start making changes to move toward a healthy, sustainable life, eliminating the things you know aren't bringing you peace and life from God.

Discussion Questions

1. Does your typical day look anything like the family in Chapter Two? Is it less chaotic or more?

2. If you look back at the list of signs of fatigue, do you see any in your life? Where do those come from?

3. Josh listed three reasons we don't rest: We have to admit we aren't God, we have to stop, and we have to know God, not just about God. Which one is most true of you?

4. Josh said, "Every time you say yes to something, you say no to something else." Do you agree with this?

5. How have you seen this truth play out in your life?

Chapter 3

Money in the Bank

I was talking to a guy who is working on his master's degree. He's married and has one child, and once he finishes his master's degree, he would like to open his own business. It's a good goal, and I'm excited for him. Then he dropped a bomb on me. "When I'm done with school, I'll have over $80,000 in student loan debt." This is going to seriously hamper his ability to start a business.

I talked to another pastor the day after this, and he explained how he felt that God was calling him to a new church. This would be a church where he would be able to use his gifts fully, where he would be happier and more passionate and more bought in to the vision. Yet the church was offering him over $10,000 a year less than his current job. He was stuck on what to do. He wanted to go, but was unsure if he could survive on that kind of pay cut.

Recently I talked with a girl in my church and she told me, "I just don't have enough stuff. It isn't that I don't have anything to wear or don't have the latest fashions; it is just that I feel like I need more than I have." When I asked her what *more* was, she didn't know. It was like asking people about balance.

Maybe you can relate.

There is a desire for more, a desire to provide, to be taken care of, to have security. Some of these desires are good and healthy; some not so much.

Money and Your Heart

Here's the big idea of this chapter: there is a powerful relationship between our true spiritual condition and our attitude and actions concerning money and possessions.

At the end of the book of Philippians, Paul says something very powerful. He has spent his entire letter calling the church to greater faith, to see how blessed their lives are and what it means to live in joy—not happiness, as happiness is a fleeting emotion that is based on what happens in our lives. Joy is something deeper, something that involves God and not just our surroundings. It is why people are able to say they are joyful in the midst of pain and suffering. It is why someone can be joyful after losing their job or getting horrible news. The joy is based on something other than what is happening.

In Philippians 4:11–13 Paul says, "I have learned in whatever situation I am to be content. I know how to be brought low, and I know how to abound. In any and every circumstance, I have learned the secret of facing plenty and hunger, abundance and need. I can do all things through him who strengthens me" (ESV).

In low situations, I know how to abound. In the moments when God seems distant. The moments I'm not able to buy everything I want. The times that the month stretches past what my bank account can handle, I can be content. In whatever situation. In the moments of plenty. When I can afford the best vacation, a night out on the town, paying off my debt, sending my kids to college, buying a car for cash—in those situations, just like the ones of hunger and need, I can be content.

The reason I said there is a powerful relationship between our true spiritual condition and our attitude and actions concerning money and possessions is that money has a way of revealing our heart. It shows us who we trust in, what matters most to us, and what is our security blanket.

I remember talking to a man who was an empty nester. He had worked hard, raised two kids, and now had grandkids, and he said that he had always called himself frugal. He stayed on budget and didn't buy anything frivolous. He went on vacation, but nothing elaborate. Then he grew silent. He looked at me with tears in his eyes and said, "I'm not frugal. I save my money not for the future, but just in case it rains and God doesn't show up with an umbrella."

Being Content

Content is something we tell our kids to be. In the month of December, kids around the world all of a sudden have a million "needs." "I need a Nintendo DS." "I need an iPad." "I need a car." You would think no one gets anything for their kids the other 364 days of the year. As parents, we shake our heads, but they learned that from watching us. If you are reading this book, you probably paid for it. Thanks for that. You are reading it with lights, a roof over your head, and maybe some music playing in the background, with your favorite cup of coffee or tea on the table next to you. What other needs do you have? Disposable income, time to read, and brain power to do so. Yet contentment doesn't work like that for us.

Our contentment often rises or falls based on what others have or what we perceive others to have, but that isn't what contentment is; that is envy. When we think of contentment, we often think of a life we'd like to have; a status we'd like to achieve; a house, vacation, or possession we'd like to be able to afford. Sometimes, our contentment goes with how we feel about our body and if we like what we see in the mirror. This leads us down the road of envy and discontentment. And the fact that we have an incorrect definition of contentment is why we don't have breathing room when it comes to our finances. True contentment, though—what Paul is talking about—is not a comparison game with the person next to you. Contentment is something different. Contentment is a satisfaction in what you have; it is peace, less stress.

My guess is that, if you are reading this book, you want to be content. You want to look at what you have and feel good. You want to live off what you make instead of going into debt to buy things you can't afford to impress people you don't like.

Why Contentment Is Hard

Andy Stanley said, and every money management book proves this true: You can't borrow time, but you can borrow money.[1] Because of this, contentment is always just a loan away. Contentment is always just a credit card charge away. One more trip, one more purchase, one more night out.

The average American has $15,000 in credit card debt, and that number continues to climb.[2] If you struggle with wanting things, a desire for comfort (and who doesn't), you will find contentment an elusive feeling. People will always have more than you; you will always see commercials that continue to tell you how you are missing out and need more than you have.

Think back to the family we met at the beginning of Chapter Two, the one with no breathing room in their schedule. As long as their schedule continues to run out of control, at an unsustainable pace, their finances will suffer. Running from one thing to the next will tax them on gas. Eating out isn't a big deal, but when it becomes a regular occurrence, it adds up. The more snacks you buy to get through the day so you can have energy for that afternoon meeting, the more it costs. If you spend $3 a day, then you are spending $15–20 a week simply to stay awake in the afternoon.

While you can't borrow time, how you manage your time will have a dramatic impact on your finances.

Which brings us back to this word: contentment.

The reason many people do not have breathing room in their schedule is that they aren't content. They feel as though they are missing out. They aren't willing to let something go. The feeling that their child needs to play a sport year-round, so that they are always at the gym, on the field, or at the track, will keep them running and their wallet getting lighter and lighter. We talk about money, health, and schedule as if they are unconnected, but they are intertwined with each other in deep ways.

Let's talk about longing for a minute. If you look at your neighbor, co-worker, sibling, or anyone else and long for what they have in terms of stuff, house, car, or gadgets, why do you do that? Maybe you were raised in a family in which that sort of status was so important to who you are that you had to have certain things. You might feel as if there is a certain level you must live at or else you will struggle with feeling adequate.

I know many men feel this not only from their parents but also from their wives. Now if you are a woman, don't worry; I'll talk about how men mess this up too. Many women can unconsciously make their husbands feel as if they aren't providing for them to the level they want. In our family, Katie is the detailed one; she majored in math and engineering in college, so she handles the bank account. We talk on a regular basis about our goals, our budget, where things are, and what things need to change to live within our means or prepare for a trip. There have been times when we've been out shopping or running errands and I'll see something I want. If it were up to me, we would have hundreds of thousands of dollars of debt, because I will buy anything, which we'll talk about in a minute. Her response most of the time was, "We don't have the money for that." Or "That isn't in the budget." Those are true statements. What I was hearing, however, was, "You don't make enough for us to buy that. If you made more, we could buy more of what we'd like."

Consequently, I was never content. I felt as if I was failing her as her husband. She never said that, she never felt that, but I heard that. This malcontent can lead to a push on the schedule to work more, take on more stress to move ahead in life, which will lead to less sleep, putting weight on (which we'll look at in Chapter

Four), and then slowly the marriage begins to drift apart and both partners get lost in fantasy worlds (Chapter Five). The slide is slow and often unseen until we aren't sure what to do about it.

So why is contentment hard for you? Do you feel pressure from your kids? Your spouse? Your boss? Your in-laws?

Now, why do you care what they think?

Many times we don't think about why we care about the opinions we care about. We just care. For years I was pushed by the opinions of my extended family. Growing up, whenever my cousins and I would be in the same place, my grandparents or aunts and uncles would ask everyone how school was going. When it was my turn, they asked me how soccer was going. My cousins made the honor roll and got scholarships for college because of academics. I played soccer. The message I heard was, "You aren't smart enough." In fact, when I was in high school, my guidance counselors told me that I wasn't college material and should look into a trade school or just get a job. I made it my mission in eighth grade to excel in college one day, and to become more than my siblings or cousins so my family would be impressed and proud of me.

I later realized something that maybe you can relate to: I will never be impressive enough to those people. Their opinion will never be what I hope it will be. They will never be proud enough of me for it to truly matter and make an impact in my life and give me what I want.

In Galatians 4, the apostle Paul is talking to a church that believed that God loved them and had extended his grace toward them through the cross and resurrection of Jesus, and that to be saved and be a son or daughter of God, they had to do nothing but take the step of accepting God's grace and acknowledging their need for it. If you are a follower of Jesus, you can relate. You can probably relate to the next part as well. The church took this grace and started following Jesus, but the people began spending their time trying to earn God's love, grace, and acceptance. There is almost this unwritten desire on our part to show God that we are worth loving, to show Jesus we were worth dying for. This often leads us to faulty thinking. *I feel like a better Christian if I do these things. If I don't do* _____, *then I'm failing God.* We in the church often associate God's love toward us with our actions, yet that isn't the case.

Paul tells them, "If you are a follower of Jesus, you are a son of God." This word "son" is crucial, even though it can sound sexist in our culture. In the first century, the firstborn son was all-important to a family. If the family only had daughters, the father would adopt a slave and make him a son, giving him all the rights of a son. While we would want Paul to say "child" or "daughter" here, it would destroy the relationship Paul is trying to highlight. In this passage, Paul says that being a follower of Jesus gives you the same rights and privileges with God that Jesus has as God's son. That is an incredible statement.

In Galatians 3:27 he also says that a follower of Jesus has put on Jesus, that we are clothed in Jesus. Our clothes are an important part of who we are; they define us in many ways and communicate our style and who we are. A follower of Jesus is one that God looks at and sees Jesus. Remember the words of God the Father in the moment that Jesus was baptized in Matthew 3: "This is my beloved Son, with whom I am well pleased" (ESV). What had Jesus done up until this point? Nothing but show up. He grew up, got baptized, and followed in the steps that God had called him to. He hadn't taught, preached a sermon, healed a person, cast out a demon, or died on the cross yet. He had done nothing of significant note, except direct his life in the direction that God the Father had called him to. This is significant, because we feel closer to God and act as if God loves us more based on what we do rather than on who God is.

But It Takes Money

I know what you are thinking. *That's great, Josh, but I have bills to pay. I have debt that I don't know how to get out of. I need money. Money is what makes the world go round, and I need it to eat, play, retire, send my kids to college, buy a car, and have a roof over my head.*

That's all true, and we'll talk more about that in a minute. But if you are insecure about where you stand with God and how God sees you, contentment will always be elusive.

I told you before about my goals to prove my family wrong and look smarter than my cousins. When I graduated college, I set my sights on getting my master's degree and then my doctorate. Most seminaries want you to have three years between college and starting seminary. I convinced the seminary I attended to let me in with a six-month break. I plowed through ninety-six credits while working a full-time job in just three years. A year later, I started working on my doctorate. I was getting closer and closer to my goal. Ironically, my goal wasn't just about my family. I wanted to become someone that other people knew about so that my extended family would hear about me from other people. It wasn't enough to be at a family gathering and have something to talk about; I wanted my family to be somewhere and hear others talking about me. For over a decade, I made school my goal and the be-all and end-all.

While planting Revolution Church in Tucson, Arizona, and seeing our family grow from one child to three, I flew back to Philadelphia twice a year to work on my doctorate. If you guessed that I was spread thin and feeling the strain of it all, you would be right. But I pushed through. Katie was gracious about it, and we pressed on to reach my goal. She knew how important it was to me.

I was 80 percent of the way done, almost to the finish line. I had completed four classes and had two to go and a dissertation to write, which I had already started. I remember her picking me up at the airport from my latest trip to my school and we drove home in silence. Then I broke the silence with words I never expected to say. "I'm done. I'm not going back to school." I thought she would drive off the road. She did pull over and just stared at me.

I remember telling her, "I don't care anymore. I don't care if people ever know who I am. I don't care if I ever get called 'Dr. Reich.' I don't care if my family is ever impressed by me or if they think I'm stupid or if they think I've proven my worthlessness by quitting school. I'm done."

When I informed my school, they offered to give me a discount to keep going and told me I could take off as long as I wanted and then come back. That was 2009, and I haven't looked back or wondered about it since.

What happened? I loved school and I loved the potential accolades that would come from it. In that year, I started to believe I was a son of God (Gal. 4:1–7).[3] I had begun learning what it means to be content with who I am in the eyes of God, not someone else, and to be content with what I had and will have within that relationship.

There is no shortage of books on money management and how to get out of debt.[4] It seems like a new one comes out every week, and someone else is on the radio or TV espousing the latest way to get out of debt. Many of them simply skip this step and jump to "Debt is bad. Get out of debt. Here's what life could be like without debt." They say things like, "If you will live like no one else, later you can live like no one else" (David Ramsey). I appreciate that, because it's true. But if that is our only motivation for getting out of debt or living within our means, that goal in life will be our god and who we serve. We will find ourselves worshiping a life that we will have one day instead of enjoying the life that we have right now in God. While this might seem like a small thing, it is actually enormous. It is the heart of it all. The reason we go into debt or struggle to manage our finances is that we don't believe God loves us. We think he is disappointed with us. Some even think God is disgusted with them. Because of that, we don't see the security we have in Christ, so we look for it in money.

Finding Security in God (Not Money)

It was interesting watching our son Judah on his first Christmas in the United States. Before we brought him home from Ethiopia, he had never celebrated Christmas or received a gift. On Christmas morning, he wasn't sure what to do. There were presents, and his siblings were excited about them, but he had this growing look of concern. We finally figured out that he was worried that if he opened another present, the ones he had already opened would go away. We have the same fear about God's grace and security.

We believe that we are saved by grace, that it is nothing that we do or earn (Eph. 2:8–10). Yet when we begin following Jesus, when we take the steps of becoming the person he has called us to be, there is an anxiety that causes us to try to earn it.

We begin to hoard.

I don't know if you've ever seen the show *Hoarders* or have ever been in the house of a hoarder, but it can be eerie seeing the life of a person who simply cannot let go of anything. I remember a woman we knew who struggled with this, who had an entire room filled with just yarn. For her to take a bath, she had to take things out of her tub so she could get into it.

While that might be extreme, we often do the same thing when it comes to money. We use other words for it: frugal, cheap, conscientious, planners, or budget-minded. And while we may be those things, if we aren't careful, underneath our frugality and savings might be a god of security that we are finding in money instead of in Jesus.

In Luke 12, Jesus tells the story of "the rich fool." This man began amassing more wealth, more crops, and he needed a place to put them. So he did what any smart businessman would do: he built bigger barns to house his crops. This is simply wise stewardship. You have more, so you need more space for it. We do the same thing as our families grow, as our businesses grow. I'm not sure Jesus is saying this is a bad thing. Yet in Luke 12:19 the man says, "And I will say to my soul, 'Soul, you have ample goods laid up for many years; relax, eat, drink, be merry'" (ESV). The good life—this is what we are shooting for. This is what happens when we live like no one else so we can live like no one else.

Before you jump all over me and begin to think I am espousing poverty theology or telling you to give away everything you have (although Jesus told one guy to do that, so don't jump too quickly), there is something important happening here that we can miss in our goal to gain wealth or get out of debt.[5]

Look at how God responds in verses 20–21: "But God said to him, 'Fool! This night your soul is required of you, and the things you have prepared, whose will they be?' So is the one who lays up treasure for himself and is not rich toward God" (ESV).

Is God against wealth, planning ahead, or savings? No. What God is against is a man who finds his security in that and fails to trust God. This man began to find security in a full barn, in being able to kick back and simply wait for the end to come. I remember talking with a man once about this, and he told me after reading this story, "I'm that guy. I call myself frugal, but I find my security in a full barn. Until I have that, I won't be content." As with all things in this book, breathing room is found when our heart is right.

Anxiety and Money

For most of us, fear, worry, and anxiety go hand in hand with finances. Because of this, when Jesus talks about money, especially in Luke 12 and Matthew 6, he also talks about worry, fear, and anxiety in the same breath. Right after the parable of the rich man, he talks about how we shouldn't be anxious. Same way in Matthew 6: he lays out how we should pray, talks about fasting, talks about where we find our treasure and our hope, and then says, "Do not worry about tomorrow."

You and I get anxious about the things we can't control, and money is something we think we can control. Although if most of us are honest, money tends to be something that controls us instead of the other way around. In our culture, money is something you can borrow, so we keep borrowing and borrowing until we get the life we think we want. This is another reason we struggle with pace—because we think we can borrow time. But we know that isn't true.

Enough

Money and breathing room become tricky because, as we know, we can borrow money. Whenever you need more breathing room, you can charge it, borrow it, or put it on layaway. At some point, though, all things come due.

Remember, those who have breathing room are the ones who choose short-term pain for long-term gain.[6]

In terms of money, that could mean choosing to not go into any more debt. It might mean choosing to get out of debt. It might be downsizing your house so that you can put more into savings or retirement, or get more involved in a ministry you've been wanting to get involved with. Often the things we are earning money for have no lasting value, but they are the things everyone else is earning money for, so we keep going. That cruise, a newer car, the latest clothes, another pair of shoes, or a new tool. At one point, Katie and I had two iPads and two Kindles. Was it nice to have these things? Sure. We told ourselves they each served a purpose, but it was also a question of enough. Was one enough for each of us instead of two?

If I'm honest, this is by far the hardest chapter for me to write. I agonized over what to share and the content it should have. It isn't because the Bible lacks things to say about money and breathing room; it is that of all the things we've talked about and will talk about, this is still my biggest struggle. I want more than the next guy. I want more shirts, a new pair of jeans from the Buckle (my favorite jean store), the newest iPad. Right now I have the iPhone 4, which means a few new iPhones have come out since I've gotten mine. I can't tell you how many times I've looked online trying to figure out how to convince Katie why I needed the 5 or the 6 Plus or whatever is about to come out.

Why?

It isn't because I don't trust God. I do. I just want more than what he's given me.

That is why the words of Matthew 6 have become more of a prayer for me to read on a regular basis. Listen to the words of Jesus:

> Therefore I tell you, do not be anxious about your life, what you will eat or what you will drink, nor about your body, what you will put on. Is not life more than food, and the body more than clothing? Look at the birds of the air: they neither sow nor reap nor gather into barns, and yet your heavenly Father feeds them. Are you not of more value than they? And which of you by being anxious can add a single hour to his span of life? And why are you anxious about clothing? Consider the lilies of the field, how they grow: they neither toil nor spin, yet I tell you, even Solomon in all his glory was not arrayed like one of these. But if God so clothes the grass of the field, which today is alive and tomorrow is thrown into the oven, will he not much more clothe

you, O you of little faith? Therefore do not be anxious, saying, "What shall we eat?" "or "What shall we drink?" or "What shall we wear?" For the Gentiles seek after all these things, and your heavenly Father knows that you need them all. But seek first the kingdom of God and his righteousness, and all these things will be added to you. Therefore do not be anxious about tomorrow, for tomorrow will be anxious for itself. Sufficient for the day is its own trouble.[7]

When I want more than I have, when I crave because I feel like I don't have enough, I am telling God, "I don't think you've given me enough. I don't think you care about me enough, because if you did, I would have more." Essentially, I'm being a whiny child.

Chances are, you do the same—either complaining to God about how someone makes more than you do or has had an easier time getting a degree or starting a business. Maybe you fall into the trap of not trusting God and finding your security in what you have and what you earn. You want to trust God and pray as if you do, but if the truth be told, you see your bank account as the account you will use just in case God doesn't come through. Not coming through on his promises, because he will do that, but coming through the way you think he should. Often those two things are very different, and when they are different, they reveal the cracks in our heart.

Breathing New Air

I would encourage you to spend some time reading Matthew 6:25–34 and 2 Corinthians 9:6–15. Look at what Jesus says in Matthew 6 and ask these questions:

- Do you believe what Jesus said?
- What is the hardest thing for you to believe in those words?
- What is the easiest thing for you to believe?
- Do you believe that God cares for you more than the birds of the air?
- Looking in your past, how have you seen God prove himself true on his promises?
- What in your past can be an encouragement to continue trusting God with what you are facing right now?

Then, spend some time reading 2 Corinthians 9:6–15 and think through these questions:

- What is your reaction to giving and generosity?
- What in your past shapes that reaction?
- What does it mean to be a cheerful giver?
- Looking at your giving, is it cheerful? Why or why not?

Discussion Questions

1. Is contentment something you see in your life or is it a struggle for you? Why?

2. Why is comparing with others so easy to fall into?

3. How is the comparison game destructive in our lives?

4. Josh talked about believers being clothed in Jesus. How does this truth change how you see what you have so that you can live in contentment?

Chapter 4

Hating the Scale

If you were to ask most Americans what one thing they would change about themselves, they would tell you something about how they look. According to *The Journal of Clinical Psychology,* two of the top five New Year's resolutions have to do with weight and body image: to lose weight, which is number one, and to stay fit and healthy, which is number five.[1]

Consider this:

- 35% of Americans are obese.[2] Experts predict this number will increase to 42% by the year 2030.[3] If this is true, the number of obese Americans will increase by 32 million people.

- An additional 30% of Americans are considered overweight.[4]
- Medical costs for obesity are over $146 million each year.[5]

Or how about kids in the United States:

- One out of three children are overweight or obese.[6]
- If a child is obese at age six, the likelihood that child will be obese as an adult is over 50%.[7]
- Children that are overweight have a 70% chance of being an overweight adult. If one of their parents is overweight, the likelihood increases to 80%.[8]

Am I Overweight or Big Boned?

I hadn't always been overweight. I played soccer year-round through my junior year of college. Being that involved in a sport covers up for a multitude of sins when it comes to eating; that and being twenty years old and having the metabolism of a four-year-old.

Something happened that year, as I began gaining weight. I quickly ballooned up to almost 300 pounds, with a 42-inch waist and a 2XL shirt size.

What was interesting about this entire situation is that I was working on staff at a church at this time and no one said anything. No one asked if I was eating too much or not getting enough sleep. No one told me that I should maybe skip the pancake breakfast or not get seconds at the next church potluck. Nothing. In fact, until I preached on this, I had never even heard a sermon on weight loss, health, eating habits, or gluttony, and the connection they have to my heart, but I'm getting ahead of myself.

It came to a head when our first child was born. I was my heaviest at age twenty-five. In fact, when they did my blood work to get life insurance, they were hesitant to insure me, and it was incredibly expensive. At twenty-five!

Around this time, Katie and I were at a friend's house having dinner. There were four couples, and I made the mistake of wearing a long-sleeved shirt. For most people, this wouldn't be a mistake, but for me it was. What made it worse was that it was a little stuffy in the house, and we had spicy food to eat. Right there at the table, I started sweating. It was incredibly embarrassing as it made me feel even heavier than I was. When you are overweight, you think someone skinnier can sweat and blame it on food, but you feel like everyone is looking at you. It was one of those moments, like the moment you discover your first zit in middle school, and the only reason you discovered it was because someone pointed it out. Or, like standing in front of a room full of people and discovering your fly is down. I was so embarrassed. I wanted to crawl under the table, but then I would have been a fat guy stuck under the table, sweating.

Since that moment, a lot has changed. I had tried all kinds of diets up until that moment, and nothing seemed to work. I would lose some weight and put more back on. I would try an exercise program, but nothing stuck.

Then, one day, something happened. It all changed. But, again, I'm getting ahead of myself.

Right now, you might be wondering if this chapter is for you. You might not be overweight or struggle with eating too much. It is for you. Let me tell you about some friends that you might be able to relate to.

Meet John. He's a friend in his mid-thirties and he works out very little. During his entire life, he has had no reason to think about his health or his eating habits. He is the type of person who can eat three cheeseburgers in a meal and not gain any weight. Each day he eats fast food for lunch. This has created a lifestyle that is not sustainable as he gets older. He confided in me recently that for the first time in his life, he is feeling lethargic after eating and starting to feel as if his clothes are getting a little tighter.

Daniel is another friend of mine. In high school and college he was in great shape, because he played sports. But then he got a job, got married, and his exercise habits slowed down. But his eating habits didn't. Now that he is almost thirty, he is starting to long for what he used to look like. If you were to look at him, you wouldn't think that he is overweight, but when he compares what he sees in the mirror to what he wants, he's unhappy.

Heather is another friend. She's single, works part time, and goes to school full time. She wants to get married one day, but has always struggled with her weight. It isn't that she eats a lot of food; she just makes poor choices about food. She wishes that she could have more time to exercise, but with school and work, it ends up being a quick bite here, a short night's sleep there, and a Friday night with friends that leaves her feeling lonely and unhappy. Whenever she sees her friends who keep the weight off and eat whatever they like (at least in her mind), and sees the women at the mall or in a magazine, she feels heavier and heavier.

I have another friend named Paul. He is overweight by about sixty pounds. He works too many hours each week, sleeps too little, and eats too much. He never exercises. He takes time to be with his family and attend church. He doesn't have a desire to lose weight or be healthier and doesn't really see the point, as it hasn't affected his health in his opinion. In fact, he would say that his weight isn't a problem and it certainly isn't a sin. When I talked to him about the content of this book, he looked puzzled and asked me why he never heard a sermon or a pastor talk about health or weight.

Lisa is another friend. She's married, in her mid-thirties, and a mother of two toddlers. She spends her days chasing after her kids and picking up after them. She's tired, but wants to exercise and get back to her pre-baby weight. She looks at magazines, which never help her feel better. They only remind her of the body she used to have. Her husband doesn't complain, but she is unhappy with the body she has now.

If we were honest, there are things that all of us would like to change about our bodies, about what the scale reads when we step on it or what we see in the mirror. It might be something in our control or something that is out of our control (like hair loss), although with technology and surgery, more and more seems to be in our control.

Measuring Up

One of the biggest struggles for many has to do with body image.[9] The statistics on eating habits, obesity, lack of exercise, stress, anxiety, and TV watching are startling and probably not a surprise to anyone, but it's what we do with the statistics that is even more alarming. Many of us vow to make a change, but it's easier to stay in our patterns that contribute to our unhealthy lifestyles. Why is that?

This makes Americans some of the unhappiest people on the planet, and much of this unhappiness has to do with how they see themselves.

According to dosomething.org, here are several facts regarding body image:[10]

- Approximately 91% of women are unhappy with their bodies and resort to dieting to achieve their ideal body shape. Unfortunately, only 5% of women naturally possess the body type often portrayed by Americans in the media.
- 58% of college-aged girls feel pressured to be a certain weight.
- More than 1/3 of the people who admit to "normal dieting" will merge into pathological dieting. Roughly 1/4 of those will suffer from a partial or full-on eating disorder.
- 95% of people with eating disorders are between the ages of 12 and 25.
- Only 10% of people suffering from an eating disorder will seek professional help.

The disparity between what we see on TV, in a movie, or in a magazine has led many people to feel like they don't match up. Yet we go about trying to get there in often unhealthy ways.

The truth is, we are striving for an *image*, not reality. Our culture and our minds have created an impossible ideal when it comes to our bodies. As I look at the men who end up on the cover of *Men's Health*, I have to remind myself there's a good chance they don't have five kids and a full-time job. Unless their job is to be muscular or skinny—then, yes, they have a job.

It is easy to look in the mirror and feel inferior, feel fat, or that you aren't beautiful. We all do it. We all play the comparison game, whether it has to do with our careers, bodies, or lives. We compare our marriage to someone else's. Our kids get the comparison treatment from us as well. We read what people put on Facebook or post on Instagram and are jealous of their lives. We so easily forget that no one posts failures on Facebook or Instagram—only successes.

I used to think that if I got healthy and got in shape, all that would go away. It doesn't. If your goal is a certain body or a certain weight, you will find yourself always chasing a weight, because you won't be skinny enough or beautiful enough. And it's a hard way to live. I know, because I have fallen into this trap when I don't remember that the goal is to be healthy and not to project a certain image.

A Good Image

On a regular basis I share my weight-loss journey with people. You might be wondering: How did I lose 130 pounds in eighteen months and keep it off?

There was a plan that I created, stuck to, and have continued to stick to that has changed my life. But something happened, and it is the one thing that many people skip in their journey to lose weight or be healthy.

By now, you can probably guess it, as we have talked about it when it comes to our schedules, pace of life, money, and other things. The question of *Why?* Why are you unhealthy or overweight? What has led to this place in your life? It doesn't just happen and it isn't just genetics. Yes, some people have an easier time losing weight and others have an easier time putting weight on.

There were two verses that I came across, which you have probably read or heard a sermon on if you have been in church for any length of time. The problem is not that you don't know these things; it is that you don't believe them and see the implications for your life.

The first verse is in Genesis 1. The creation of all things. In this passage, we see the reason for existence, God's plan for all things, and his plan for you and me. If you read Genesis 1:1, it says, "In the beginning God created the heavens and the earth." D. A. Carson said, "If you can accept Genesis 1:1, the very first verse in the Bible, then you really won't have trouble believing the rest of the Bible." This verse is the crux of it all, and it sets the stage for what we are about to learn.

As you read through Genesis 1, you see this rhythm of God creating all that we see out of nothing. In our culture, being created, creation, and existence mean something is material, something is there, it takes up space, or we experience it. In the ancient world of Mesopotamia, when Genesis was written, something existed if it had a role to play. Meaning, if something was created, then it had a purpose; it was not accidental. One of our struggles with our bodies and finding freedom as it relates to body image is that we don't believe we were created with a purpose or a role to play. We get frustrated with the size of our nose, our hairline, waistline, hips, the size of our hands or feet, or how tall we are, yet this was not accidental.

Keep this in mind as you read this next verse: "Then God said, 'Let us make man in our image, after our likeness. And let them have dominion over the fish of the sea and over the birds of the heavens and over the livestock and over all the earth and over every creeping thing that creeps on the earth.' So God created man in his own image, in the image of God he created him; male and female he created them."[11]

The God of the universe creates us in his image. Remember, when it says *created*, what the writer of Genesis is saying is "with a purpose and reason for existence."

There is more happening here that I don't want you to miss.

The word *image* refers to containing the essence of something. *Likeness* is connected to substance, resembling something. Much as an older relative may have told you while you were growing up that you look just like your dad or just like your mom.

In Scripture, when the word *body* or *image* is used, it refers to a whole person: mind, body, heart, soul, and strength. The whole person. When we think of body and image, we are too narrow in our thinking, and this narrowness keeps us from feeling fulfilled as we are.

Lastly, when God created things in Genesis 1, he said, "Let there be." When he created Adam and Eve, he said, "Let us . . ." His creation of us is incredibly personal, purposeful, and caring.

This might be hard to believe. The God of the universe, personally creating you with care and a purpose. The closeness of God to us in our creation is astounding and so often missed.

Dominated

The next one is a verse that Christians love to quote when it comes to things like smoking or drinking, yet the implications are bigger than that. Paul is writing to the Corinthian church, and he tells them, "'All things are lawful for me,' but not all things are helpful. 'All things are lawful for me,' but I will not be dominated by anything. . . . Do you not know that your body is a temple of the Holy Spirit within you, whom you have from God? You are not your own, for you were bought with a price. So glorify God in your body."[12]

The first implication is this: What dominates you? For many people, food dominates us. We do not view food as fuel; we view it as an escape. For many, food is what they turn to when they are stressed, life feels out of control, they are tired, or need comfort. For many, it is an addiction.

Think about the last time you felt really stressed, really tired, or life felt out of control. You may have been at home or at work, but you can picture it. You know what happened and who was involved. What did you do in that moment? There's a good chance, if food is an issue for you, that you grabbed something to eat. It might have been a donut, a whole meal, or a pint of ice cream. We'll look deeper at this in Chapter Six, but one of the reasons you are not healthy, living the life you were called to live, is that you see food as a god.

The other thing Paul points out in this passage is what your body is. We saw in Genesis 1 that we were created with a purpose, a reason for existence. Paul tells us that our body is the temple of the Holy Spirit, bought with a price. In this passage, he lists all kinds of things that can destroy the body and tells us that we were freed from these by the cross and resurrection of Jesus. Food is a spiritual issue. This verse is often used by Christians to say, "Don't smoke or drink too much" as they stuff another Big Mac in their mouth or eat a third piece of pie at the church potluck.

Turning Point

For many, the idea of wondering or discussing what God thinks of our bodies rarely enters into the conversation.

I think one of the main reasons is that many pastors are unhealthy. When I was at my heaviest, I had a talk with my brother-in-law that proved to be a life-altering conversation. We were at Starbucks and he asked me, "How can you challenge people in sermons to have self-control when you don't have any in the area of food?" I'll admit, the question caught me off guard.

The reality of being overweight in the Christian community is that until you have a heart attack or some other health issue, no one will say anything to you. It isn't seen as a sin, so what's the point of saying anything? If you choose to be overweight, it's your choice. But, as we'll see in a minute, I believe many people—skinny or overweight—are sinning in the area of food and body image.

The larger issue is one my brother-in-law pointed out: pastors are unhealthy and many of them are overweight. A 2001 Pulpit and Pew study of 2,500 clergy found that 76 percent were overweight or obese compared to 61 percent of the general population at the time of the study.[13] We'll see more in the next chapter about what this stems from, but for many pastors (and leaders in general), it has to do with a lack of controlling their schedules when it comes to their sleep and exercise habits, along with making poor choices at their lunch meetings, or laziness. I think the larger issue for people who say they believe in God is that we compartmentalize the gospel to the point that it is strong enough to save us for eternity, but not strong enough to transform our eating habits or body image issues.

But it's not just pastors who are overweight; the problem has moved into the pews. A 2006 Purdue study found that fundamental Christians are by far the heaviest of all religious groups, led by the Baptists with a 30 percent obesity rate compared with Jews at 1 percent, Buddhists and Hindus at 0.7 percent. This study prompted the lead researcher, Ken Ferraro, to say, "America is becoming a nation of gluttony and obesity, and churches are a feeding ground for this problem."

Similarly, a 2011 Northwestern University study tracking 3,433 men and women for 18 years found that young adults who attend church or a Bible study once a week are 50 percent more likely to be obese. The Pawtucket Heart Health Program found that people who attended church were more likely than nonchurch members to be 20 percent overweight and have higher cholesterol and blood pressure numbers.[14] Why is this? Why are we more prone to these things than those outside the church?

The answer to that question has to do with the other reason that churches don't talk about food as an addiction, exercise, or body image issues. That's because it can be awkward. I didn't realize this until I lost all my excess weight. I remember standing on stage talking about this, weighing in at 170 pounds and looking out at my church. Then I saw some people who were overweight, some who were very obviously overweight, and others who were just slightly overweight. Whenever you bring up weight, body image issues, or food as an addiction, immediately everyone thinks you are talking about someone who looks overweight. While you are speaking to them, it goes beyond each individual, and leaders must see it as a larger issue as well. It isn't that we as pastors want to shame anyone in our church or any leader wants to make someone who works for them feel guilty. But we know they will feel so much better about themselves and their life if they can gain the freedom that Jesus offers in this area. We want them to experience the life Jesus promised. Too often, we interpret this life described in John 10:10 as simply being about heaven. Or we think in terms of money and careers. This life, an abundant life, is also about the pace we keep, what we put into our bodies, and how we think about our bodies.

A New You

When we think about the scale, our weight, body image, or making a New Year's resolution connected to this, we think of a new you.

Can you relate to my story or to any of the people we met earlier in the chapter? For you, food may not be an addiction, but something you mindlessly turn to. Food may be something that controls your life just as drugs control someone else's life.

Before we move forward with some action steps, I want to ask a question you may have never thought about before: Is food, body image, or your health a heart issue, a sin that you need to confess?

You cannot breathe new air, you cannot find freedom in your life without answering these questions. Many times we simply want to grab the latest diet, the latest workout plan, and hope for the best. If you haven't discovered it yet, it isn't that simple. If it was, everyone who spends millions of dollars on health-related products would be skinny. It isn't a lack of want; instead, it is a lack of heart change.

I know you will feel tempted to push through this question and read what comes next, but if you do, my fear is that you will be back in this same place a year from now and still be miserable with what you see on the scale or in the mirror.

Breathing New Air

Okay, here are six things I would tell you as you move toward a healthy lifestyle:

1. **Make it the next thing on your schedule.** This is crucial. Put working out on your calendar. Currently, I work out four or five times a week. I put my workouts into my calendar each week. They are a scheduled appointment, like the dentist or a meeting. When the time rolls around (whether that is 6 A.M. or 5 P.M.), it is simply the next thing I'm doing. Over time this has helped me to get up and go to the gym. Believe me, I can fill that time with something else, but it's a commitment I've made. The reality for many people is that they aren't willing to give the time it will take to be healthy.

2. **Pick a plan you like and will stick to.** It doesn't matter if you ride a bike, run, do CrossFit, Zumba, or something else.[15] Pick something you will do and stick with. Too often I'll see people switch plans or programs because they don't see changes quickly enough. When I started working out, I saw a ton of changes fast. Then I went almost two years where I thought I looked the same, but I stuck with it. In the past three months, I have seen more changes than in the previous fifteen months combined.

3. **Set a realistic, attainable goal.** Set a goal. Be specific. With a deadline. Now, is it realistic? If you do nothing right now, working out four days a week at 5 A.M. probably isn't the best first step. Maybe try two times a week at that time, and then build up. Get small wins as quickly as possible. Exercise goals are like getting-out-of-debt goals; if you can start hitting a few, you get excited and want to keep going.

4. **Eating well is more important than exercising.** This is something most people miss. Eating counts more than working out. Don't kill yourself at the gym and then go home and eat like a guy living in a frat house. Eat well. Remember, food is fuel, and according to 1 Corinthians, it matters what you put into your body. If you exercise regularly, you should drink at least 100 ounces of water a day. Limit dessert and other foods that aren't great for you. You don't have to cut out gluten like I do,[16] but eat well.[17]

5. **Weight gain isn't always a bad thing.** If you lift weights, this will be something you need to learn. I stopped weighing myself three months ago. Our scale's battery died and I never replaced it, so it wasn't a conscious choice, but it has been a good thing. Weight gain is not always a litmus test for being unhealthy; sometimes it indicates muscle growth. Muscle does weigh a lot. Have a pair of pants that test whether your waist is growing.

6. **Health is a lifestyle switch.** Don't quit. Being healthy is a long-term choice. Sure, working out feels good, but

I also do it to stay healthy for Katie and my kids, and to have energy to lead well. I want to stay in the game well into my eighties.

Which of these resonates with you the most? Do you need to wrestle with the heart issues of food, weight loss, and body image?

What is your goal for the next month, and who is going to hold you accountable for it? If you want, shoot me a tweet (@joshuareich) to let me know your goal and make it public. I'd love to see you complete this and share your success story!

Discussion Questions

1. How does the truth that you are created in the image of God affect how you see yourself and your body?

2. Read 1 Corinthians 6:19–20. What dominates your life? Is what you put into your body honoring God?

3. Of the six points listed at the end of the chapter, which seems the easiest and the hardest for you to do to have a healthy lifestyle?

4. Which of the six points resonates with you the most? Do you need to wrestle with the heart issues of food, weight loss, and body image?

5. What is your goal for the next month, and who is going to hold you accountable for it? If you want, shoot Josh a tweet to let him know your goal and make it public.

Chapter 5

Your Imaginary World

Hopefully by this point, you are beginning to see what has held you back from having breathing room in a number of areas in your life.

If we're honest, one of the reasons we don't have breathing room is that we long for a different life. It isn't that our life is terrible. You may have a good life. A job that isn't terrible (if you want to feel better about your job, just watch an episode of *Dirty Jobs*). Your marriage isn't all that it could be, but it is there; you have someone to come home to that you like. You aren't the wealthiest person you know, but you have what you need.

If we aren't careful, though, our fantasies can drive us. Not necessarily sexual ones, although as we'll see in this chapter, that might be the case. Our fantasies, longings, and daydreams drive much of what we do. They drive what we shop for, the debt we take on, the pace we live at, and they just plain drive us.

When we lack breathing room, our fantasy world is where we turn to relieve stress. We also turn to our imaginary world because it is easier than dealing with something or working on a relationship.

If you attend church, there is a good chance you will never hear anything about this. It isn't because your pastor doesn't think it's a sin; believe me, he does. It is just uncomfortable to talk about. Talking about and confronting issues like drinking, politics, debt, and fighting in marriage are easier to tackle, less uncomfortable.

Let's lay out first why there's discomfort. First, many pastors and leaders struggle with their own sexuality, addictions, past hurts, and fantasies. Statistically speaking, 40 percent of pastors struggle with porn addiction.[1] For many leaders, this is hard to talk about, because they are in the midst of the struggle. Pastors also battle daydreaming and fantasizing about a different life, a different marriage, different circumstances and problems. For many, it feels hypocritical to talk about it.

Second, when it comes to your body, sexuality, and "private" addictions, it gets incredibly personal. It is easier to stay focused on the more public sins.

The World That Doesn't Exist

We all have a world that doesn't exist. It might be a world in your head that you go to on really tough days. It is the world where your ideas work. It might be a persona that you are on Facebook, but not the real you.

Maybe for you that fantasy world is porn or romance novels. And yes, I think they are the same, as we'll see in a minute. Russell Moore puts it like this:

A new book by Boston University researchers Ogi Ogas and Sai Gaddam, *A Billion Wicked Thoughts*, offers a disturbing look at how Internet search engines reveal much about the sexual and emotional desires of men and women, and how they differ. The research confirms in some ways what almost everyone knows: men are visually engaged, attracted to youth and sexual novelty, and are thus vulnerable to visual pornography.

The research explores further what the commercialized romance industry tells us about what it means to be a woman (at least in a fallen world). Women are much less likely to be drawn to visual pornography (although more do so than one might think), but are quite likely to be involved in . . . Internet romantic fiction or the old-fashioned romance novel.

The romance novel follows, the researchers argue, a typical pattern. The hero is almost never a blue-collar worker, a bureaucrat, or someone in the traditionally feminine occupations (hairdresser, kindergarten teacher, etc.). He is competent, confident, and usually wealthy. He is, in short, an alpha male.

But, they argue, this alpha male is typically a rough character who learns to be tamed into kindness to her. Thus, you wind up with not only the strong silent cowboys with the soft interior life, but also these days vampires and werewolves and Vikings.

And all of this is moving toward the climax of the romance story: the "happily-ever-after."

"Romance novels rarely have a sequel," the book concludes. "Once the hero and heroine are joined in love or matrimony, they get their Happily-Ever-After, presumably with a bevy of children and domestic bliss. Further adventures would violate the female fantasy of true, committed, eternal love."

While I don't share all the presuppositions of these scholars, I think they're on to something about the allure of the commercialized romance story. Pornography and romance novels aren't (or at least aren't always) morally equivalent, but they "work" the same way.

Did you catch that? They work the same way.

The problem is, "Both are based on an illusion. . . . Men want the illusion of women who look just like women but are, in terms of sexual response, just like men. Women want the illusion of men who are 'real' men, but, in terms of a concept of romance, are just like women. In both artificial eros and artificial romance, there is the love of the self, not the mystery of the other."[2]

Because of the Internet, magazines, and movies, we have become desensitized to sex and have become so used to our fantasy worlds that it no longer bothers us that they aren't real. These fantasies no longer faze us, so many times we don't wrestle with whether they are right or wrong, or even if they are doing any damage to our minds, hearts, bodies, and souls. Fantasizing is simply something we do, as normal as sleeping.

The rise of reality TV, being a voyeur in someone else's world, has become accepted and exciting. We share photos on Instagram and Facebook of our kids or the meal we just made. We pin things on Pinterest of projects we plan to work on at home, but more than likely will never get to. We want people to believe something about our lives—not what they are, but what they appear to be. This in turn causes us to kill ourselves to get a certain life, because we see the life we think others have.

One of the reasons fantasy worlds are so dangerous is, not surprisingly, they aren't real. I remember seeing someone post on Facebook one morning, "I'm so in love with my wife, she's so hot." What made this curious was that two days before that, I met with them because they were on the brink of divorce. They wanted the façade of a great marriage for those around them to see.

Our imaginary worlds are so dangerous because we mindlessly slip into worlds where we don't have to put forth any effort, worlds that are solely about us. Now, I understand completely the desire to unwind after a long day—to sit down, catch your breath, and relax—but there is danger in switching our minds off and simply being mindless in our desires. Think about it like this: Have you ever found yourself sitting on your couch watching TV or clicking on Websites on your iPad and looked up to see it had been three hours? You were just bored and found yourself zoning out on things.

There is something deeper that happens in our imaginary world, and that's what I want to spend our time on in this chapter. Our fantasy worlds are a litmus test of what is going on in our lives.

When a man is addicted to porn, it reveals several broken places in his life.[3] A man is not addicted to porn in isolation. Most men I meet who struggle with porn have things broken in their past. It might be abuse, many sexual experiences, a lack of appropriate affection while growing up, or an inability to handle the stress of life. In the same way, when a couple is not engaged in a healthy intimate life, it shows problems in other areas. When a couple is in a rough patch of their marriage, sex and affection are often the first things to go. It becomes a litmus test for the rest of the marriage. Women struggle with opening themselves up to their husbands because of past abuse, hurt, a lack of trust, or a struggle with body image. Men have a hard time engaging appropriately with their wives because of porn, selfishness, stress, or just because of how tired they feel. Sex and affection simply become too much work, but our imaginary worlds are always there for us.

The question of this chapter is, *If your fantasy world is one that is more attractive and exciting than your real life, what does that reveal?*

Define Your "Other" World

What is your other world? Is it the false pretense you put on of who you wish you were? What you wish others would see? If we looked at your Facebook profile or your dating profile, would it be accurate?

Is your fantasy world getting wrapped up in romance novels because that is the best it will ever get? Maybe you find yourself lost in a world of porn. It is where you go for comfort, for approval, and to have a woman look at you through that screen and smile.

Before you think this is an easy battle for me to fight or something I've never walked through personally, let me pull the curtain back for you.

When I was eleven, I went to a sleepover for a friend's birthday party. Innocent enough. Four of us in the sixth grade always hung out together. On this night, my life would change forever. We were in my friend's basement; we'll call him Ian. We were playing video games, and Ian's dad walked down into the basement with a box. He put the box on the ground and said, "It's about time you boys started to learn about this, so here you go," and walked upstairs. The four of us paused the game and went over to the box. Inside was something I had never seen, something I didn't even know existed. Porn. Ian's dad apparently was a collector. He had magazines, calendars, and videos.

This night changed my life and had an impact that I still feel twenty-five years later. It began a ten-year porn addiction that I couldn't shake. I tried everything: accountability groups, accountability on my computer, reading books, running, taking cold showers, memorizing verses. I agonized with God, crying out that he take this temptation from me, but to no avail. No matter what I did, I couldn't stop. It became an all-encompassing desire for me.

I doubted my salvation as I found myself repenting over and over to God in hopes that he would save me and that if I died, I wouldn't spend eternity in hell. I was gripped by the guilt and shame of this. I walked around with the fear that other people knew and yet didn't say anything. I was afraid of what people would think if they knew my inner struggle, the angst that kept me awake at night, the desire that drove much of my life. For me, looking at porn was a daily activity.

During this decade in my life, I went to Bible college, was on staff at a great church, and I got married. I hoped that all of these things or one of them would help this addiction to go away. The harder I tried and the more I tried, the worse it seemed to get. In the midst of this struggle, I struggled alone.

Even marriage didn't help. This is a myth many men believe—if I get married, I'll stop looking at porn. The reason, as we'll see in a minute, is it never gets at the disease and sin in your life; it only tries to treat the symptoms. When Katie and I got married, she had no idea. In many ways, I wanted her to find out in hopes that I would find freedom if she knew or could help me figure it out. Whether consciously or not, I began leaving clues in hopes she would find out. For me, this was my last shot at victory before giving up. It wasn't fair to her, but I didn't know what else to do.

I still remember sitting at work and getting a phone call from her. On the other end of the phone she was crying and silent in a way that was not normal for her. Katie is outgoing, caring, and fills a room with her personality: one of the things I love about her. This phone call was different. At first, I thought someone had died. The reality was, someone did die, and it was Katie.

Addictions, particularly private ones that involve our minds and fantasies, can be very destructive. That's because they are private. They become things that run our lives. For me and for every other person I've met who is addicted to something, whether it is porn, shopping, food, gambling, or smoking, it runs them. It controls schedules, thinking, feelings, and how we see the world and ourselves in it.

There's a good chance you are shaking your head right now. You might be thinking, *I'm not addicted. Sure, my profile picture is from when I was thirty pounds thinner, but I'm not addicted to it.* But would you actually be able to take down that photo that makes you look better? The reason many of us think we don't have a porn addiction, a romance novel addiction, a perception addiction online is because we imagine what an addict is like. An addiction is a *persistent, compulsive dependence on a behavior or substance. A person who is addicted to a particular substance. An enthusiastic devotee of a specified thing or activity.*[4]

Let me give you another word to use: "dependent" or "compulsive." Do you find yourself dependent on one of the things listed above? If you don't look at Facebook, play a video game, or look at porn, will you find yourself stressed out? Can you make it through a day without them? What about simply doing them without thinking? This is where compulsion comes into play, when we find ourselves simply doing them. How often do you find yourself checking Facebook without thinking, ignoring those around you? In the end, you may be closer to this being a problem than you think you are.

The Me I Wish I Was

If we were sitting together for a meal and I asked you to describe your ideal self, detailing the things you wish weren't true about yourself, you could do it. You might focus on something physical: the amount of hair you have, the length of your arms, how wide your hips are, or how flat your stomach is. You might talk about your past, things that you wish were no longer there and things that, if taken away, would make you feel better. You might talk about abuse in your background or pain that has gone unhealed for decades. You might mention an addiction that has plagued you for what feels like a lifetime. Shopping, debt, food, cutting, pornography, never being alone, a desire you have to control everything, or how fear plagues you at every turn. We might focus on things that were said to you as a child, destructive words that told you that you weren't good enough, smart enough, and beautiful enough. Maybe it was the absence of words like, "I'm proud of you. I love you. You are worthwhile."

All of us have an ideal picture in our mind, but the reality of our past often keeps us where we are. Our ideal self is complete, beautiful, attention grabbing. At the very least, it is not who we are. This picture, this incompleteness that we all sense, is what drives our addictions. It is what drives our sins and our fantasy worlds.

There is something else that goes into our ideal selves, and that is the world and lives we imagine that others have. At every turn, we are bombarded, through TV, our children's schools, magazines, Facebook, and our friends; we are told that we don't measure up.

It wasn't until I got a Facebook account that I realized what amazing lives my friends lived. They cook great food, have great drinks at Starbucks, their kids are cute, and they are always checking in some place. How do I know? They take pictures and tell me. They have so much fun without me.

Have you ever seen someone post a picture of an ugly child on Facebook? Check in somewhere and say it was horrible? Maybe they've burned dinner and then Instagrammed a picture of that? I have never seen that either.

This standard that we put forth online, that our friends put forth, pushes our image of what an ideal life is. It makes us want it more than what we have. Everyone has more fun than we do, they have incredible date nights, are in love with their spouse, their kids are cute and don't misbehave, and as we read, we go deeper and deeper into the pain of what we wish were true about us.

Relationships That Elude Us

Because of our fantasy world, relationships often elude us for a couple of reasons. One might be because we spend all our time in a fantasy world, so we don't know how to have relationships or community with real people. Community is crucial to finding freedom from food and the other things that hang us up in life.

Recently, I gave up Facebook for Lent. According to *Christianity Today*, that is a common thing to give up, ranking 19th on a list of the top 100 things people give up at Lent.[5] What I learned over that time is how fake much of my community was. I relied on social media to tell me when my friends had birthdays, what they were up to, and what things they liked. If you think about it, you probably do the same thing. We don't have to ask our friends what movies or books they like; just look at their Facebook profile to see what they "liked." We don't have to talk with them about their day, because if we read their Facebook wall, we will know what they did that day, what they ate, and who they were with.

There is another reason relationships elude us when it comes to our fantasy worlds, and that is because we aren't free yet. When we aren't free, we don't present our real selves. When we don't present our real selves, we don't let people in, and we don't let them get close.

As we talked about before, one of the reasons you have a fantasy world or a secret addiction might be to deal with some pain you carry around. It might be abuse at the hands of people who were supposed to love you, protect you, and care for you. Instead, they used you. It was easier to get lost in something to numb the pain rather than face it.

Maybe you lost someone very close to you at a young age, and it rocked your world. It will never be the same. No matter how hard you try, you can't seem to move forward. It is just too hard.

Maybe you were married and your spouse (in front of your family, friends, and God) said he or she would always be with you and love you no matter what: rich or poor, in sickness and in health. It didn't matter how much old age and gravity affected you, you'd be together. But they didn't. Maybe she cheated on you, maybe he got lost in porn, or maybe she or he just walked away. And no matter what you do, that pain just won't go away. You can't seem to find a way to move forward. You are not alone.

I talked to a woman named Susie the other day, who told me that even after five years, she couldn't stop thinking about her ex-husband, how he cheated on her and how much it still hurts. Through her tears, she told me how she throws herself at any relationships just so she won't feel alone.

Maybe you have a hard time trusting people. Why should you trust them? Everyone you have ever trusted has done the same thing: stabbed you in the back and walked out.

This is why we get lost in a fantasy world. It is easier. No matter what you or I do, that girl on the computer screen will always look excited that we are there. That guy in the romance novel, the one who says all the right things and has the washboard abs, will be there no matter what we look like.

This is why fantasy is so much easier than real relationships. We don't have to let our fantasy relationships into the deepest places of our heart. They don't care that we don't open up or that we don't share our hurts or our hopes. It doesn't bother them that we haven't dealt with our baggage.

Making Someone Else Pay for Our Past

Right now you might be thinking, *You have no idea what I've been through. All you've wrestled with was a porn addiction.* It's true. I haven't suffered abuse. I haven't had a spouse walk out on me.

I have had close friends stab me in the back. Soon after we got married, I was on staff at a church. It was a good church, but it wasn't a good fit for me. I shared my feelings with my boss, thinking I could trust him. He was encouraging and asked some good questions, but he told me to keep wrestling with God about what I was called to. During this time, he took those questions to the leadership of the church. I quickly found myself out of a job.

It was years before I trusted someone I worked with. I remember the day it happened. When I started Revolution Church, I was a part of everything. When you start a church or a business, it is like another child. We hired a worship pastor named Paul soon after starting. From day one it was obvious that Paul had a lot of gifts outside of just leading worship. The problem, though, was that I didn't trust him. Why should I? The last guy I trusted had hurt me. Paul didn't do it, and he shouldn't have had to pay for the sins of someone else, but he did.

Thankfully, Paul was patient and Jesus worked on my heart, and I was able to see the brokenness of how I was living. I also got to see how my brokenness led me to hide, to not let go of things, and to not trust. I learned a lot from this experience, and needless to say, it deeply affected my physical and emotional health.

Being Okay with the Person You'll Never Be

It is hard to move forward to breathing room in this area of our life. Many of us don't even know who the "real me" is or what we would be like without an addiction to porn, romance novels, fantasies, video games, or posting our ideal (but not real) life on social media.

Even after I realized that I could trust again, the issue of my physical health still plagued me. And from what I experienced then to now, there's something we all have to realize at some point. The bodies you see on the screens, in the magazines you look at, and in the workout and weight-loss books you buy, there's a good chance you will never have that body. And we need to be okay with that.

I remember reading about the workout rhythms of some of the biggest actors in Hollywood and what they ate. Guys that were followed around by a personal chef who made everything perfectly, just the right amount of protein, and how they worked out six hours a day.

As a father of five kids, I don't have six hours a day to spend at the gym. I don't have a personal chef that follows me around. I need to eat healthy on a budget while having lunch meetings at restaurants and spending too much time at Starbucks.

Part of the fantasy that we live out is the fact that we don't think realistically about our lives. Now, it is possible to get that body. You need to remember what we learned in Chapter Two: *when you say yes to something, you say no to something else.* If you say yes to working out even two hours a day, there will be a host of things you'll have to say no to because of time. But we need to look at what we are doing to achieve the body we would like to have. Is it to be healthy or to gain what can come from having a body that everyone notices? Our motives are often an indicator of what we really believe about what is important to us. And our motives show what we believe about Jesus and if he really is all we need.

I had a friend who was dieting and had to eat specific things from the company that created the diet. Because of this, he never ate with anyone. He couldn't go to someone's house for a meal. He missed many relationships and many opportunities to grow as a leader and a husband. He said yes to his health, that's true (although it was a diet that was probably impossible for anyone to maintain), but he had to say no to many other things. He missed the crucial idea that our plan for being healthy must be something that is sustainable and a long-term solution which doesn't take us away from the life God designed us to have with others.

Truth be told, you may never have those pectoral muscles, the veins in your arms, or the calf muscles you crave. Ladies, you may have those stretch marks and loose skin from your pregnancy for the rest of your life. You may never get back to your pre-baby weight. Years will pass, and you will start sagging in the wrong places. But it's okay when you are healthy and you realize that the physical things you crave aren't worth the price you have to pay for them.

You may never be the best cook or have the most romantic moments to post on Instagram, but it's okay to miss the opportunity to take a great picture of your kids for Facebook because you are focused on actually spending time with your kids. Your Pinterest board may be nonexistent, but you have a home filled with love and grace that is captivating to those who enter it.

The Freedom We Long For

I remember a night that was one of the low points in my journey. I couldn't seem to find freedom from food or porn. I failed at both that night. I sat there in front of my computer. At this point it was off, so I could see my reflection in the screen and I wanted to cry. But I couldn't. I was just so sad, so deflated, and so hopeless.

One verse that I've always come back to is John 10:10, where Jesus says why he came. He says, "I have come that [you] may have life, and have it to the full." In that moment, as I sat there and thought about how broken my life was, that verse came to my mind.

This thought occurred to me. If I believed that Jesus really was who he said he was, and if I really believed that Jesus was life and that he came to give me life, then anything not named Jesus would not be life.

You probably know this. I knew it; I just didn't live it.

Many of us live as if our sins are better than Jesus. I lived as if being alone and not letting people get too close so they couldn't hurt me was better than Jesus. Every time I looked at porn, I said with my life, "This is more satisfying, more comforting than Jesus." Whenever my life felt out of control and I turned to food to feel better, I said with my life, "This food will bring me comfort, more comfort than Jesus ever could." Whenever we feel stress, pain, hurt, or loneliness and we turn to anything other than Jesus, we have moved into sin and away from freedom and life.

Likewise, if you get close to forgiving the person who hurt you and you decide not to forgive them, you are saying, "Holding back forgiveness and being angry is better than being free in Jesus." It isn't easy, but you are already on the journey by spending time with a fellow sojourner, and often this first step of admitting you want to change is where most people won't go. So stick with me. I really do believe this is possible for you if it was possible for me.

Not Held Against You

Romans 8:1 says, "There is now no condemnation for those who are in Christ Jesus."

I had read this verse before, but it wasn't until recently that I began to understand what this means. When Jesus died on the cross in my place, he took my sin upon himself, dying the death I deserved. He took all my condemnation, all my sin, even before I committed it.

What that means is if you are a follower of Jesus, Jesus paid for all that pain and baggage that you carry around. God no longer sees it. You are no longer that hurt little girl in his eyes; you are a woman who has been redeemed and can experience freedom. You are no longer that man who can't control himself. You are a man who has been redeemed and no longer has to find fulfillment selfishly, but can control himself through the power of Jesus.

When we get to the place that we don't think of this as a fairy tale, something too good to be true, we will understand what Jesus meant in John 10. We will begin to see life for what it really is: life.

The life you and I settle for is not life. We settle. We keep people at arm's length, give in to temptations we know we don't need, all in an effort for a moment of comfort, a moment of forgetting about the pain. But that isn't life.

Protecting Your Family

If you are a parent, you live with fear about your kids. I have a daughter and four boys; and I am not naïve about the world they live in and will walk into. Many parents take one of two approaches when it comes to their kids and potential addictions: throw up their hands and give up, or batten down the hatches and wait for Jesus to return.

I would submit that neither way is the wise way to go.

I know that my boys and our daughter will one day encounter pornography, beer, R-rated movies, cigarettes, food, body image issues, the desire to fit in, and feeling that they don't measure up.

As a parent, my role is to help them prepare for this moment and to be someone they can turn to. Not as a friend, but as a parent. I want to be friends with my kids, but not like the ones they hang out with, because I'm still their parent.

This means I can't fall asleep at the wheel in terms of culture and what they are listening to and watching. I must continually scour blogs and social media to stay up on what they are encountering. I need to know about movies before they do and what is in them. If I'm unsure, I watch it with them or before them.

The reality is, our kids will go out of our house and encounter a world without us.

This is where wisdom comes into play, as we teach our kids and prepare them for this moment.

For our family, this means a couple of things. First, we don't do sleepovers. I can tell you, this is one of the least popular decisions in our children's young lives. It is good practice for when we will disappoint them as teenagers. We don't do it. How many lives are destroyed at a sleepover? Through movies that are watched which leave scars that heal but slowly, or abuse at the hands of a parent, a sibling, or even the friend who invited them over. As I shared in my story, my life was completely changed because of a simple sleepover that I still feel the effects of.

Second, we talk with our kids about media, culture, style, dress, language, and other things as they come up. We talk about the worldview of the people who create culture and art. We talk about what makes people write what they do in movies, wear what they have on in magazines, and what was behind the creation of a video game. This is teaching our kids how to think critically about the world around them. Our goal is to help them be discerning instead of simply taking in entertainment and culture.

Often when men find out we have a daughter, they put their hand on my shoulder and say, "Good luck." I tell them, "Thanks, but the way I look at it, I have an eighteen-year head start on any punk coming along." It is the same with my boys. I'm here before everything else they will encounter. Do I have more power over those forms of entertainment? I'm not sure, but I know my voice can be loud and forceful if it needs to be.

Never underestimate the power of a parent or grandparent who chooses to be involved in the life of a child.

Lastly, pray for them. My wife and I continually lift up the lives of our kids. We pray for their future spouses. I pray for the men in the lives of their future spouses because of the enormous impact men have on young lives. I pray for the women my boys will marry, that they will be strong and soft, that they will have a desire to love them as men, not as boys or with a romantic love the way a woman defines it. I pray that my daughter will marry a man who will help her love Jesus more and make every effort to pastor and lead her well.[6]

Don't throw your arms up or batten down the hatches on your life or the lives of your kids. Whatever you face personally or as a family, you can get through. Jesus walked out of a grave on the third day when his disciples had lost all hope.

Breathing New Air

Now that I've shared my story with you, the hurts that led me to spend years addicted to porn and its effects, take some time to look at your life. Do you find yourself addicted to porn, romance novels, an online life, a fantasy world? Do you find yourself doing it compulsively and without thinking?

If so, what is your game plan to fight it?

How will you train your kids to fight this temptation? Statistically, the first time a boy sees porn is at eleven years old, and many teenage girls struggle with looking at porn. Many parents want to pretend it isn't real or ignore it, but it is real. Do you have a plan to fight this in your family? We will look more at this in the last chapter of the book, but for now, I want to get you thinking about creating a plan and wanting to have a plan that is more than wishful thinking.

In short, I want you and your family to experience life. That's what we've been talking about for the last four chapters: life and what keeps us from experiencing it.

What does life look like, though? Turn the page and let's start talking about that life, how I got there, and how you can get there too.

Discussion Questions

1. Do you have an imaginary world that is affecting your real world?

2. Where did that imaginary world begin?

3. Why do you find yourself drawn to it even when you know it is wrong?

4. Do you have a secret addiction that you need to find freedom from?

5. What is your plan to find freedom that will last?

Chapter 6

Why You're Gasping for Air

For all of us, something or someone runs our lives. Hopefully over the course of the first five chapters, you have begun to see what it is. My goal so far has been to help shine a light on some of what is keeping you from living the life you are called to live, the areas where you have no breathing room. More than likely, it didn't surprise you. You already knew you were too busy and spent too much time fantasizing and daydreaming. If you are in debt or you let shopping or things run your life, you knew that. If you struggle with body image or weight, you already knew that as well.

I hope that isn't all that has happened so far. I hope that you are beginning to see *why* those things have such power in your life. Why your past is so scary to face, why you struggle to face what you have done or what has been done to you. I hope you are beginning to see why you are running so fast and far from what you've lived.

I hope you are beginning to understand where your addictions come from, why freedom has always eluded you. To see how you have idolized the next stage of life—the dream of getting married, having kids, having the kids move out, moving into the next part of your life—instead of enjoying the place God has you right now.

Or you might be seeing why you are just unhappy. Why you always seem stressed out, miserable, and just downright sad.

At this point, if you and I were having coffee together or we were in a counseling session at my church, you might ask, "What now?"

In most churches, in most counseling sessions we would look at the sins in your life. We would talk about your addiction to porn, your willingness to give your heart and body away in relationships, the pace that you keep, how you go into debt buying stuff you can't afford, how you always gossip, or why you push yourself and your kids to be the best and attain a certain kind of lifestyle. We would then immediately jump to what to do and how to stop doing those things.

If you've ever tried this approach, you know it doesn't work. We can't simply change our behavior and see lasting change. Until we understand *why* we do something, change and freedom will continue to elude us.

Finding Meaning in Sin

The book of Ecclesiastes is one of the most interesting books in the Bible. If you've never read it, here are the CliffsNotes. The writer of Ecclesiastes is called the Preacher. It might have been Solomon, but we aren't sure. We do know that the Preacher was wealthy, had a lot of land, buildings, crops, money, and servants. He had influence, the life that people long to have. Yet he was miserable.

The book of Ecclesiastes is written at the end of the Preacher's life, and he looks back on what he accomplished, the search for meaning that he went on. He searched for meaning in sex, in building, land, jobs, money, career, relationships, and food and wine. You name it, he tried it.

Yet he came up empty.

Three thousand years after the book of Ecclesiastes was written, you and I still try to prove the Preacher wrong. "He may not have been able to find meaning in running from one thing to the next, but I will. He may not have found meaning in relationships and giving his heart and body away, but I will. He may not have found meaning in food and wine, but I will."

We don't say this, at least not out loud. But when we sin, we do so out of a desire to find meaning. We sin from a place of emptiness. We sin from a place of wanting to be filled up. The search for meaning drives many of our decisions, and ultimately it's the driving factor in our search for breathing room.

The Idol You Worship

Every time we sin, we do so because we don't believe Jesus is truer or better. At that moment we believe that sin will bring us more happiness, joy, and satisfaction. We sin because of something.

Maybe you've seen the emptiness that comes from simply trying to stop something. It is impossible because you haven't uncovered the root cause. You can get rid of the effects of the mold or the mildew in your house, but until you fix how it gets there, it will just come back.

Our sins are the same way.

Have you ever been to a buffet—one where the plates are stacked, and whenever you pull a plate off, they all move up? Think of your life and sins as being like that stack of plates. Most of the time when we sin or hear a sermon, it is about the plate on top. To see true change, to see the things that crowd out our lives get conquered by the power of Jesus, we have to keep pulling up plates until we get to the last one. What we'll call *the sin under the sin*.

Here are a few questions to uncover what that is for you. As we go through them, take some time to write down your answers.

- What is the first thing on your mind in the morning and the last thing on your mind at night?
- How long does it take you to check Facebook in the morning?
- Do you daydream about purchasing material goods that you don't need, with money you don't have, to impress people you don't like?
- What do you habitually, systematically, and undoubtedly drift toward in order to obtain peace, joy, and happiness in the privacy of your heart?
- When a certain desire is not met, do you feel frustration, anxiety, resentment, bitterness, anger, or depression?
- Is there something you desire so much that you are willing to disappoint or hurt others in order to have it?

- What do you respond to with explosive anger or deep despair?
- What dominates your relationships?
- What do you dream about when your mind is on idle mode?
- What, if you lost it, would make life not worth living?

What came up while reading through those questions? Do you find yourself daydreaming about people liking you or accepting you? Do you find yourself checking to see how many people liked your Facebook update? Do you have a desire that you have to fulfill every day?

I talk to a lot of guys who tell me they are addicted to porn, masturbate, or cheat because a man "has needs." My response to that is, "Have you ever heard of someone dying from a lack of sex? Ever been to a funeral, and when you asked why they died, the answer was, 'It was crazy. All of a sudden Bob's wife stopped having sex with him, and he just died.'" No. Many of the things we put in the "need" category—sex, shopping, work, adrenaline—are not needs but desires. Many of them are good desires given to us by God that are corrupted by our sin.

That last one is a crucial question. The answer to the last question will begin to uncover the idol that drives your life. Idols in our hearts are the things we worship and serve instead of Jesus. They are the good things in our lives that we make great and ultimate.

What if you lost your job or your house? What if a relationship ended? What if your business closed?

For example, we love our kids. I can't imagine the devastation of losing a child. I've sat with parents who have, and as a father, it scares me to think about such a thing. But if losing a child would make life not worth living, what does that say about my view of Jesus? What does that say about how I have elevated the view of my kids in my life?

Now, here is what you will learn about your idols. They are usually not bad things. My kids, my wife, my job, pastoring, writing, working out, spending time with friends, going to the beach, taking that dream vacation, watching my Steelers play, enjoying a great cup of coffee or a good bottle of wine—good things.

They become sins when we make them ultimate things. They become sins when we put them ahead of Jesus. They become sins when we look to them to give us our identity, to give us hope, to meet our needs and make us happy.

We buy into this thinking often in our relationships and our careers. Everyone can quote Jerry Maguire saying, "You complete me." When couples get married or are engaged, if you were to ask them why they are getting married, they might tell you the other person completes them. "I can't imagine my life without them." This is a good thing, but it can also reveal the brokenness in our hearts.

Our lives quickly become connected to this identity. We find our identity as Bobby's mom, as Julie's husband, as the business owner, as the teacher, as the guy who works out, as the person with the cool house, as the Bible guy, or the woman who is put together.

If we aren't careful, what is good in our lives quickly becomes the defining aspect of our lives. When that happens, we believe a lie.

Sadly, this is easier than you might think.

The Driver

I'm not very good at golf. I want to be. I like the idea of golf and the idea of being good at golf. Every golf bag has a driver. This is the club you use when you want to hit the ball the farthest. You use this to get the most bang for your buck. This is the ultimate club, because it covers the most ground.

Each of us has a driver in our lives. This is the thing that pushes everything else forward. It is different for each person.

Let me give you an example from my life. I love control. I love to make plans, to know what is going on, to know details. This makes me feel in control and needed. Now, it is easy to excuse this and say, "That is being organized. Someone who starts a church or a business should do that." Which is true. But that isn't why I do it, at least it's not all of the reason why I am this way. When life would feel out of control, I used to eat. I found solace and comfort in food. Now I can quickly find peace in a good workout. We'll talk in the next chapter about how we trade sins, so hold on to that thought.

Maybe for you, the sin beneath the sin is a desire to be approved. You want people to notice you, to compliment you, to be impressed with you. This is why you throw parties, keep a spotless house. It's why you push your kids to get straight A's, to be the best on the team. Not because you want them to succeed or have a great life, although you'll say that, but because if they don't, you are worried about how that will reflect on you as a parent.

Maybe the sin beneath the sin for you is comfort. You want to have things, be comfortable, live on a nice street. I remember talking to a guy who told me, "Jesus could take everything from me, but not my house. If he asks me to give up my house, we'll have words." For him, providing for his family was not the goal;

having comfort was. That is what he worshiped, what was ultimate in his life.

The sin beneath the sin for you might be power. You push to be the best, to always win. Not just to accomplish the American dream and have the life your parents never had, but a desire to be number one. There is no mountain too tall, no challenge too tough. You have to be the smartest in the room, the most accomplished on the team, and you want people to know that about you. Conversations and attention must always turn toward you.

The Last Plate (The Root)

Have you named your plate? Do you know what is on the bottom of your stack of plates?

Name it. Don't just breeze through this. The concept, this idol, is what is crowding your life out. This idol is what is keeping you from freedom and breathing new air. This idol is what is keeping you from living the life God created you to live, the life Jesus came to give you.

It is not enough just to name the last plate; we have to know where it came from.

Why do you try to control things? Why do you try to get power? Why is comfort so important to you? Why do you want to be noticed and get people's approval?

Maybe your drive for approval comes from never feeling that your parents or a teacher approved of you. You always heard, "Why can't you be more like your sister?" You felt as though someone else in your life succeeded while you lagged behind. You never heard your parents say, "I love you, I'm proud of you." Your life has become an endless cycle of getting that affirmation.

Maybe your drive for comfort comes because your parents didn't have much and struggled financially, so you want to make sure that doesn't happen to you. You don't want to find yourself or your kids lacking something as you did growing up.

Maybe your desire for control comes from a life that always felt out of control. A roller coaster ride of broken relationships, trust that was broken, and emotions that ran all over the map. You don't want to fly by the seat of your pants. You want to know the outcome before you start a project; you want to keep everyone in line. Maybe you grew up in a home filled with shouting, and so your desire for control comes from a desire for peace in life.

Maybe your desire for power comes from a sense of entitlement. You've had things handed to you your whole life, and you deserve to be at the top. You don't have to work for things in life; you get them handed to you. Your dad continually told you, "Don't be a loser. I didn't raise a loser." So you push. You work harder and longer than everyone else. No sacrifice is too big to make so that you don't lose.

I have a drive to win in all that I do. It isn't so that people will approve of me, but so I will feel like I have arrived. It is this inner bar that I have set up for myself. It stems from hearing teachers tell me I was behind. In middle school, they put me in slower classes; my guidance counselor in high school told me college wasn't for me—so I have this drive that continually pushes me.

It wasn't until I began to understand what was underneath it all that breathing room was even possible. It's the same for you: until you do the deep dive to understand what the bottom plate is, breathing room will always be a mirage, something off in the distance.

Why Breathing Room Is Almost Impossible

If you are like most people I talk to about this concept, right now you are thinking, *This sounds nice, but I'm not sure it's possible.*

My wife Katie was recently talking with another woman who's married and has two kids. She was lamenting about all that she is trying to accomplish, what her husband is doing, and all that her kids were into at that moment. She wanted time to exercise and time to eat dinner as a family. She was carting her kids from activity to activity and struggled to keep her house clean, and her husband was busy as well.

Katie asked her what she was going to do.

Her response was one I've sadly heard hundreds of times, and it used to be my response: "What can I do?"

The short answer Katie gave her is, "A lot."

As Greg McKeown said in his fantastic book *Essentialism*, "If you don't prioritize your life, someone else will."[1]

If you are feeling hopeless about your life and how over-crowded it is, as this mom was, there is a good chance you have allowed others to prioritize your life. It might be a boss, a parent, an in-law, a sibling, your child, a neighbor, the president of the PTA, your spouse, or your elder team.

Fear of Saying No

Think for a minute about the last time you said no to someone. Can you remember when it happened? If you have to think about it very long, then you are reading the right book. All of us have a desire to please people on some level. For some, it is because we want to be nice or be liked; for others, it is because we find a lot of identity in what others think of us and how they perceive us. We don't want them to not like us. We don't want to come across as mean, and saying no feels mean. In fact, one author said, "In our society, we are punished for good behavior (saying no) and rewarded for bad behavior (saying yes)."[2]

There is a fear that I have in saying no. It is the fear that I will miss an opportunity.

Last year, our neighbor told me (in front of our two oldest boys) that he had just signed up his son (who was the same age as my oldest son) for tee ball. He wanted to know if we were going to sign up. I was stuck. My two sons wanted so badly to play tee ball with their friend. I also remembered starting to play soccer when I was four, and I thought this would be a great idea. After all, most professional athletes started playing their respective sport at four or five, which was the age of my two sons. So we signed up for tee ball. We were at the field three nights a week and every Saturday. Did I mention my sons were four and five? Absolutely ridiculous.

On top of that, my sons weren't learning anything. I had worked with my sons, so they were further ahead in their ability than the other boys, and while teamwork and helping others are great lessons to learn, on a tee ball team no one is learning those lessons.

My fear of my sons not getting a baseball scholarship because they started playing too late or disappointing my sons in front of their friend and this other dad caused me to suck all the breathing room out of our family for three months. By the time the season ended, we were gasping for air.

Choices

Peter Drucker said,

> In a few hundred years, when the history of our time
> will be written from a long-term perspective, it is likely
> that the most important event historians will see is not
> technology, not the Internet, not e-commerce. It is an
> unprecedented change in the human condition. For
> the first time—literally—substantial and rapidly grow-
> ing numbers of people have choices. For the first time,
> they will have to manage themselves. And society is
> totally unprepared for it.[3]

When I read this the first time, I stopped in my tracks. Drucker said this in 2005, and in 2015, it is even truer. We are unprepared for the choices we run into. Whether at school, work, church, for hobbies or activities. Options and choices seem endless. We can get every-thing in any color, whenever we want. This unprecedented reality causes many of us to gasp for air. Couple this reality with the truth that many people allow others to prioritize their lives and our fear of saying no because we fear we will miss something or ruin our kids. We run from one choice to the next, never bothering to slow down and ask if this is the best thing to do.

Remember: *Every time you say yes to something, you are saying no to something else.*

Fear God and Keep His Commandments

What's behind our fear of saying no? Is it the fear of missing out on something or the paralysis that comes from too many choices?

I believe our fear comes from learning that our meaning and hope will not be found in those things. Not only will breathing room elude you, but meaning will as well. We'll look deeper at meaning and how to achieve it with breathing room in Chapter Ten. It is something we all want. We want our lives to count. We want what we do to matter. We want our existence to have a purpose.

After all the searching for meaning, at the end of Ecclesiastes we learn where meaning can be found. It isn't in our idols, our desires, food, sex, relationships, work, stuff, land, houses, or addictions. We are told in Ecclesiastes 12:13–14, "The end of the matter; all has been heard. Fear God and keep his commandments, for this is the whole duty of man. For God will bring every deed into judgment, with every secret thing, whether good or evil" (ESV).

When the Bible talks about fearing God, it doesn't mean that we are to be afraid of him or be tentative with him. It means that we are to worship him, that he is to be first in our lives. When we worship the idols of control, power, approval, and comfort, God is not first in our hearts. You might think this idol talk seems silly. Why not just deal with the sins we can see?

The writer of Ecclesiastes tells us that our actions will be judged, along with our secret things, the things that people can't see. Those secret things are the idols of our hearts.

When we confront the sin beneath the sin, the sin that keeps us from worshiping God first, we are able to find freedom and keep his commandments. We can do what he calls us to when we give up our need for power, control, comfort, and approval. We can live out the commandments he has given to us in Scripture.

I love the sense this verse gives us. Often when we think about commands, we think about things that God wants us to do for his pleasure. But obeying God brings him pleasure in the same way a parent has pleasure when a child listens. Following God's commands, just like a child listening to a parent, is for our good, for our pleasure, for us to experience life. His commands aren't bondage; they are freedom.

Breathing New Air

Write this down. My sin is _____, which comes from the sin underneath the sin that is _____.

What truth about Jesus don't you believe when you commit both sins?

Tim Chester, in his book *You Can Change,* has four simple truths that have helped me to preach the gospel to myself when I find myself worshiping my idol. They are:

1. God is great—so we don't have to be in control.
2. God is glorious—so we don't have to fear others.
3. God is good—so we don't have to look elsewhere.
4. God is gracious—so we don't have to prove ourselves.[4]

Discussion Questions

1. Josh said, "When we sin, we are looking for meaning." How have you seen this to be true in your life?

2. After looking at the questions in this chapter on pages 112 and 113, what is the default idol of your heart (power, control, approval, or comfort)?

3. What is the root of that idol? Where did it come from?

4. How do you see this idol play out in your life on a regular basis?

5. Which of the four gospel truths (the 4 Gs) at the end of the chapter is the one you need to preach to yourself on a regular basis? Which truth are you most likely to not believe?

Chapter 7

The Vending Machine of Sins

In the last chapter, we looked at some of the lies that we believe. You've probably learned by this point, through this book and your own life, that you won't find freedom until you uncover the sin under the sin.

I remember the first time I preached this at my church. I got more texts and emails, and had more conversations with people afterward than any other sermon I've ever preached. Facebook comments lit up like a Christmas tree. It was as if the proverbial light bulb came on for many people.

I understand the feeling. The first time I began to figure out where my sins came from, where my addictions came from, what caused me to crowd my life out, things became a lot clearer.

I want to throw up the caution flag for a minute.

It is easy to get gung ho right now as, maybe for the first time, you are figuring out why you do what you do. For the first time, you know why you have trouble trusting people, why you buy things you can't afford, why you struggle to let go of things from your past and forgive people. Maybe you are uncovering the addictions that have controlled your life for years and discovering why they have so much control over you. But be careful that you don't trade one struggle for another.

Trading Sins

I want you to imagine a vend-ing machine for a minute. You walk up to it, put your money in, and begin to decide on your selection. Instead of coffee and candy, this vending machine has sins as the options.

At the top, you have the big ones: theft, murder, porn, drugs—things that can destroy you. Ones that you've heard pastors tell you to avoid over and over. You start to move down toward the bottom (you know, where the gum is in a

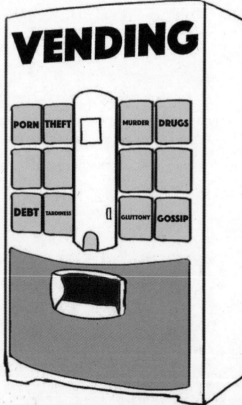

vending machine), and you have debt, gossip, tardiness, overworking, skipping children's practice, gluttony, anorexia.

The sins closer to the bottom you will rarely hear about in a sermon. People won't make many Bible studies on them—Jesus said very little about them—but they are equally sins and equally destructive.

Many people, in an effort to be holy, to appear holy, or just to make themselves feel better, choose the sins at the bottom. They rationalize that they no longer sleep around, but now they can't trust people and enter into true community. A dad no longer looks at porn, but now he can't control his temper with his wife and kids. You don't work as much, but now you are struggling to find meaning and enjoy life because soccer practices and helping with homework is not as exciting as climbing the corporate ladder.

I shared in Chapter Five about my addiction to porn. From the time I was eleven until I was twenty-one, porn was a daily struggle for me. I was embarrassed, ashamed, and I felt guilty every time I would fall into it. I tried accountability groups, accountability software, taking runs, making vows to God. Even after I got married, it never seemed to go away.

If you were to rank sins in the church, many people would put porn up at the top as one of those sins you should avoid. It is destructive and causes enormous pain to you and those around you.

When I turned twenty-one, something started to change for me. I started to look at porn less and less, but I was eating more and more. At one point, I ballooned up to almost three hundred pounds when Katie and I got married.

I chose eating too much.

At this point, I was excited. I was no longer looking at porn. The problem was I was still sinning. I still believed lies, still crowded out my life, and didn't have breathing room.

The difference was that I felt less guilty and, interestingly, while I put on weight, no one said anything. I was congratulated by my accountability group for not looking at porn, and I felt like I was on my way to life. Sinning less does not equal life, especially when sinning less is simply trading for a sin that seems less destructive or that no one talks about as a sin.

I still chose sin. I still chose an idol.

This is where much of the talk about freedom and addictions gets off track for many people and why they feel like failures in the end.

Yes, through the power of God you have conquered an addiction like debt, eating too much, working too much, or looking at porn, but you don't feel whole. You don't feel like you are living life. Something is missing.

You give up one thing, but maybe you substituted something else from the vending machine of sins that so many of us find ourselves standing in front of each and every day. You have simply made another choice. Often, that choice is a sin that is less destructive, more acceptable, or less noticeable.

Choosing Life

There is also an option in the vending machine labeled life.

This causes you to stop, because you remember that Jesus said in John 10:10 that he came to give us life. That is the reason for the gospel, the hope we have.

If you have traded sins, as we often do, Jesus's words in John 10:10 about having life to the fullest seem like a far-off mirage. Instead, your life feels like the other description in that verse: killed and destroyed.

What is missing?

This is why it's so important to understand the sin under the sin, the thing that drives you to sin.

We all want life, but few actually choose to walk down that road for this simple reason: we choose sin instead of life because we know where it leads, what the road will be like. Life is out of control and will take us to places we know we should go to but aren't sure we want to. If I choose anger, I know what my life will be like. I know where debt, greed, and not trusting people will get me. I know how it will feel and what I'll be like when I get there. I am unsure of how things will go if I trust someone, or if I walk away from temptation instead of giving in.

Trusting Jesus for Life

Life is a hard choice to make. The reason I know is that few people seem to make it. We are content to take the easier path and choose a sin.

When Jesus talks about coming to bring us life in John 10, he does so by using the image of a shepherd. This might be weird for you to understand; after all, you don't look out your window and see a lot of shepherds.

In the first century, shepherds were very common. For sheep, a shepherd provided protection. The shepherd took the sheep to food and water, showed them where the grass was, where to sleep, and while the sheep slept, the shepherd kept watch and slept at the gate.

Jesus says that he is the good shepherd.

"Good" carries the idea of righteous, trustworthy; a benefit to someone, and having the qualities needed for a particular role.

This is crucial to the choice between life or our idols.

The reason many people do not choose life is that they don't see Jesus as trustworthy, as a benefit, or having the qualities needed for what he promises. They look at their lives, their idols, and their desire for meaning, and choose another option in the vending machine of life. They don't choose the way of Jesus.

I get it; trust is hard to come by. Promises were made to you and broken. Marriage vows were not kept; a person trusted to protect you abused you instead. A promise of money and a job was taken away. A secret that was entrusted to someone was posted all over Facebook and destroyed you.

The idea of trusting anything to Jesus can be a leap for many people.

What about him being righteous? You can point to people you looked up to, respected, considered righteous, only to find out that they weren't. Pastors who can't stay pure, bosses who took advantage of you and failed to give you that bonus. It might be a spouse who failed to be faithful to you.

I think for many people, while trust and righteousness are roadblocks to choosing life in Jesus, it is the other two that trip them up: "a benefit to someone" and "having the qualities needed for a particular role."

In the moment of temptation, in the moment of desire, we don't see the benefit of choosing life instead of our sin. We only see what we want. As we sit at the computer late at night and the desire to look at porn comes, we don't see the benefit to purity, only the desire we have. When we face the temptation to take a shortcut at work and not have integrity, we don't see the benefit of integrity, only what comes from taking the shortcut and how we can get ahead.

When we face our child wanting to be on three sports teams, after-school programs, the Bible studies we signed up for, the work hours that we have to keep, we don't see the benefit of slowing down and doing less, only the feeling that if we don't do all this, we will miss something. What will we talk about if we have a family dinner every night? Will we sit there in silence? That doesn't feel like a benefit, but activities do.

We have gone so long without life that we no longer know what it feels like or the benefits that come with it.

Because of all that, we are unsure if Jesus will deliver on his promise. What if Jesus does what my spouse, parent, or boss did? What if Jesus fails to deliver as my idol does? We run this over and over in our minds.

I think this is why Jesus calls himself the shepherd and those who follow him the sheep. It will take trust on our part to find life.

Life in the Father

Trust is easy to write about, but hard to put into practice. In the same chapter in John, Jesus tells us one more reason to trust him: he and God the Father are one. In John 10:27–30 he says, "My sheep hear my voice, and I know them, and they follow me. I give them eternal life, and they will never perish, and no one will snatch them out of my hand. My Father, who has given them to me, is greater than all, and no one is able to snatch them out of the Father's hand. I and the Father are one" (ESV).

This passage is incredibly crucial to finding life, but also incredibly difficult to swallow. For the simple reason that trusting God as Father is a hard pill to swallow.

It's been said that every man and woman carries a father wound. After more than a decade as a pastor and counseling people, I can tell you that is true. Our earthly father, if he is around, shapes so much of our lives. He shows us how to view money, work, relationships, and roles in marriage. He shows us how to view God. When I talk about God as Father, your first picture of God as a father is probably very similar to your earthly father.

Look at those words from John 10 again. Jesus said that he knows those who follow him, who trust in him, who choose life over idols. He gives them life, and no one will snatch them out of his hand. Then, Jesus says he is God and God the Father, the one that many struggle to trust and follow. Jesus says that we are one: *As my sheep, as my follower, you are not only in my hand, but you are in my Father's hand. And no one can snatch you out of his hand.*

If there were one truth I could get into your head, it would be this.

The reason is simple; the implications of this are far-reaching. We go searching for meaning because we don't trust that meaning is found in Jesus. We go searching for relationships because we don't believe Jesus is trustworthy and fulfilling. We work too much to impress a man (our father) we will never be good enough for, when our heavenly Father already loves us and has forgiven us by sending his Son to die in our place.

Being a Son (or Daughter)

Ephesians 1 has to be one of the most incredible passages in the entire Bible. In that book, Paul is showing the church in Ephesus, and us, what our identity is, who we are. Many of us look for someone to name us. We want to know from an early age that we are worthwhile, that we matter, that we can be someone, that we are important.

Paul writes in verses 3–10:

> Blessed be the God and Father of our Lord Jesus Christ, who has blessed us in Christ with every spiritual blessing in the heavenly places, even as he chose us in him before the foundation of the world, that we should be holy and blameless before him. In love he predestined us for adoption, as sons through Jesus Christ, according to the purpose of his will, to the praise of his glorious grace, with which he has blessed us in the Beloved. In him we have redemption through his blood, the forgiveness of our trespasses, according to the riches of his grace, which he lavished upon us, in all wisdom and insight making known to us the mystery of his will, according to his purpose, which he set forth in Christ as a plan for the fullness of time, to unite all things in him, things in heaven and things on earth. (ESV)

The picture here is incredible. We were orphans. Lost, destitute, hopeless.

We've adopted two boys, one domestically and one from Ethiopia. The moment that you meet an orphan is overwhelming. I remember holding our son in Arizona when we met him.

He was two days old, weighed five pounds, and looked a little like Benjamin Button with all his wrinkles. The reality of what lay ahead for him in the state system if we didn't adopt him was so sad to think about. No, we didn't rescue him or save him, but we did adopt him and make him one of our family.

I remember the moment we landed in Africa to meet our son Judah. The brokenness of the country, the poverty, the smell, was overwhelming. The sense of helplessness you feel and the desire to do something, anything, is great. Judah was four when we met him and not excited about meeting us. I'm sure he had seen families come into the transition home who didn't take kids home. He certainly saw families come and go while he stayed put. So he was unsure about who we were and if this was for real.

It took over an hour for him to even look at us. Even when we would get down on one knee to be at his eye level, he wouldn't look at us. We spent a week with him, loving on him, playing games with him, hoping to communicate that "We love you and we are here for you." Then one of the worst moments of our lives happened.

We had to leave.

For some reason, the policy for adopting in Africa meant we had to take two trips. I will never forget the look on his face as he began to understand that we were leaving, and in his four-year-old mind, we weren't coming back. We tried to communicate with him through the translator, but he just looked at us with his big eyes and cried. Not a soft cry but screaming. As I carried him back to his room, he clung to my neck for dear life. As I tried to hold it together and be tough, Katie was falling apart. It was one of the worst moments of my life.

I remember getting back into the van with the other adoptive families (we were the only ones leaving that day), and they asked how we were doing. I know they were trying to be helpful, but I wanted to shout at them. Our flight home was one of the quietest plane rides I've ever experienced, as Katie and I sat there completely run-down emotionally.

How do you tell a four-year-old who only knows one word in the English language ("fish," because we brought Goldfish crackers to eat) that we are coming back? That we don't know when—it could be four weeks or six months—but we will be back. I wanted to shout at the top of my lungs in his language, "We're coming back!" Even as the workers tried to comfort him and tell him, he just continued crying and reaching out to us so that we would take him with us.

I remember when we got off the plane and we got to the hotel, I asked Katie if she wanted to walk around or get something to eat, and she said, "I just want to sit here and cry."

This is the struggle we have in trusting our heavenly Father. We were all orphans before Christ. We know the feeling of being left. We know the feeling of being forgotten. We know the feeling of being looked over, of not being chosen.

This is why Paul chooses the words he does.

God chose you. As a follower of Jesus, God chose you.

When?

Before the foundations of the world, before creating anything, God chose you.

He chose you so that you could be blameless and holy before him.

"But how?" you ask.

In love.

This love is different from the love we see in movies or read on Hallmark cards or listen to as we slow dance to a song. Love in those places is a feeling, an overwhelming, uncontrollable feeling. This is why people say things like, "You can't choose who you love." None of that is true. Love is not an overwhelming, uncontrollable feeling. Think for a minute, what if God loved you with that kind of love? What if God's love for you was a feeling, where he said, "You can't control who you love"?

God's love, the love we are called to have for those around us and in our relationships, is a choice, followed by a feeling. God chose you in love.

For what?

Adoption, as sons (and daughters) in Christ, according to the will of God. This was and is God's plan. This was not unexpected for God. The idea that Jesus would die in our place and rise from the dead was his plan.

Why?

Because we are sinners, because we are lost, because we are broken and can't fix ourselves, and because we are orphans.

Every time I read through Ephesians 1, I am overwhelmed by the love of my Father in heaven. I stand in awe that he loves me as he does. That he would go to the lengths that he did to save me and give me life.

How to Trust God

Maybe you still struggle with this question, "Can I trust you, God?" After all, when we sin, we are telling God we don't think we can trust him. This is a question everyone has; in fact, it is the same question Abraham had in the Old Testament.

If you've grown up in church, you know the story of Abraham, and our knowledge of his story kind of takes away some of the amazingness. In Genesis 12, we have this man named Abram. He all of a sudden appears in the pages of Scripture. He is out in the desert and he hears a voice. A voice he may have heard before, but maybe not. We aren't told. This voice, God from heaven, tells him to pack up what he has and move "to the land I will show you."

Now picture this: Abram goes home and tells his wife Sarai that they are to pack up and go to a land that this voice (God) will show them. I always wonder what that was like. If she was like most wives, she probably asked him how long he's been hearing this voice. Has it said other things? Did it give any directions? Any hints on what lay ahead?

No, Abram would tell her. Only that we are to start walking and stop when he says.

What God does tell Abram is that he will one day be a great nation and that all the people of the world will be blessed through him. The irony of this is that Abram has no children and is seventy-five years old.

Finally, as he walks to this land, there is a fascinating promise given to Abram in Genesis 15. Time has passed, and Abram and Sarai still do not have a child. From their perspective, they are not any closer to being a great nation than when they left their home. So Abram does what we would do. He whines to God. Complains, actually.

God takes it and is incredibly patient with Abram through this entire conversation. As Abram unloads his feelings of despair, lack of faith, anger, and hurt over his desire to be a father, but yet not having this desire met (are you beginning to see the connection between not trusting God and giving in to temptation or other sins?), God tells him to look to the heavens and number the stars. Abram can't number the stars, as there are too many of them. "So," God tells him, "shall your offspring be."

God doesn't just stop there. He tells Abram what he (God) has done. What is interesting to me is that when God gives commands in Scripture, in particular the Ten Commandments in Exodus 20, before giving a command, he reminds the people of what he has done. God is about to make a covenant, a promise with Abram, but before he does, he reminds Abram of what he has done so far. He hasn't just led him to a new place and promised him a son; he has guided, provided, and protected him and his family.

Then and only then does God give commands or make cov-enants. In Exodus 20, before giving Moses the law, he reminds him, "I am the LORD your God, who brought you out of the land of Egypt, out of the house of slavery" (20:2 ESV). This is the foundation of the commands of God, his promise and the freedom that he provides.

In Genesis 15, after reminding Abram, he makes a covenant with Abram. We aren't told in Scripture if Abram asked for it, but he was at least doubting and wondering if this was going to happen. He was complaining to God, as we would do. This has always been a comfort to me, that God doesn't strike down questions in the Bible, but listens and answers them.

God tells Abram to bring him a heifer, a female goat, a ram, a turtledove, and a young pigeon. Abram did, and cut them all in half. In this time period, when two people made a covenant, they would kill the animals and cut them in half, and then they would walk through the animals, saying, "If I don't keep my end of the covenant, may I end up like these animals."

It was getting late and Abram fell asleep. Then God made a covenant with Abram, while he was asleep. As the sun set and it was dark, a smoking fire pot and flaming torch passed between the pieces. Abram never passed through the animals; only God did.

This is the extent to which God goes to keep his promises as our Father. He makes the promise and keeps it, even when we don't. Even in our moments of failure, doubt, and fear, he is still strong and sure.

Breathing New Air

I want to invite you to take a deep dive as you think about God as your Father. What immediately comes to mind when you read those words? Is that hard to believe? Do you have an easy or a hard time trusting God?

When you look at Jesus, do you see the good shepherd who provides protection and gives life? Or do you see someone who makes you wonder if he is up to the task of keeping his promises?

Discussion Questions

1. Have you seen the truth of trading sins in your life?

2. Has that happened recently? Explain.

3. How does viewing God as a good and gracious Father change how you view and desire things that are sinful?

4. How does God viewing you as his child because of what Jesus did change your view of God and yourself?

Chapter 8

Letting Go

If there's one thing about your life you could change, what would it be? Is it something you feel guilt, shame, or regret about?

Maybe you grew up in a broken home—living with parents who didn't like each other and you got caught in the middle. Maybe your marriage is not what you thought it would be. Maybe there is abuse in your past. You've tried to move past the hurt, but it is still there, and trusting others is hard for you. Right when you are about to get close to someone, you pull back because of how people you once trusted turned on you.

What about temptation and desires? All of us have things we are tempted by, desires we wish we didn't have. Sometimes they are dark and destructive. Others may appear harmless, but still they drive us.

The truth is that we all have guilt, shame, and regret from our past. But what can we do about it so that it doesn't drive our life or drive the life out of us? For many people, their past, left untouched, becomes a compass for their future.

Our past is one of the hardest issues to deal with when it comes to finding more breathing room. As soon as we start to change and get closer to new life, it seems we are reminded of our past. As soon as we feel the exhilaration of more freedom, something reminds us of who we were . . . or, maybe more accurately, who we *think* we still are.

I've already shared about my food addiction, which lasted several years. Today, thankfully, I am in the best physical shape of my life. However, not a week passes where I don't catch myself looking in the mirror and thinking that I still see that overweight, 300-pound man I believe I've left behind.

Why do I do that? Why does the past seem to have so much influence over us?

The Drive of Guilt, Shame, and Regret

Whether we realize it or not, our past—including our guilt, shame, and regret—drives much of our life, in the present and the future. More than we'd want it to. In Chapter Six we looked at how we feel about our worth and how to find meaning in life. I want to return to those topics, because our "stuff" from the past has a significant influence on how we evaluate ourselves. Accurately, that is. We can say a lot about our past and who we are today, but we tend to be overly critical of ourselves, which is not how others see us. Not only that, but our struggle to let go of guilt, shame, and regret can leave us gasping for air—and we may not even know it or realize the tight grip it has on our heart, soul, and mind.

Look again at this evaluation: *My life has meaning and I only have worth if . . .*

- I have influence over others (power).
- I am loved and respected by _____ (approval).
- I have a particular pleasurable experience or quality of life (comfort).
- I am able to get mastery over my life in the area of _____ _____ (control).

What do our responses say about where we place our expectations for what we hold near and dear to our hearts? You'll notice that these speak to most of the things you and I experience and desire: control, approval, comfort, and power. Is there really breathing room apart from these things? To some of us, it seems about as likely as finding treasure in our backyard. After all, this is the life you have built. Who or what could take it away?

As you move toward more breathing room, you will find your past coming back to squeeze you. For most of us, it's hard to let go of the past because it has defined us—it is all we know. We become attached to our experiences, the feelings we've felt, the addictions we've struggled to overcome, the pace we've kept that made us comfortable—all because we are used to these things. We know what these things feel like—we don't know what putting them aside would feel like. And then we would be responsible for moving forward and living ahead of our past—not simply using excuses for why we act the way we do. Now that seems like a novel idea, right? Start living out of who we are now—not who we were then, the person we were before we decided to make some changes. Why do we have such a hard time simply starting over?

Perhaps letting go is difficult because we struggle to really believe God's grace and forgiveness can make a difference in our lives. Or, more often, we struggle to forgive ourselves.

A Remarkable Wedding

Maybe it will come as a surprise, but a fascinating story about a wedding will shed light on how we can let go of shame, guilt, and regret from our past.

Early in the book of John, we learn about Jesus's early life, but he is quoted very little. Jesus hasn't announced who he is or done much ministry. But in John 2 Jesus performs his first miracle, a very memorable one at that. Here is the whole account:

> On the third day there was a wedding at Cana in
> Galilee, and the mother of Jesus was there. Jesus also
> was invited to the wedding with his disciples. When
> the wine ran out, the mother of Jesus said to him, "They
> have no wine." And Jesus said to her, "Woman, what
> does this have to do with me? My hour has not yet
> come." His mother said to the servants, "Do whatever
> he tells you." Now there were six stone water jars there
> for the Jewish rites of purification, each holding twenty
> or thirty gallons. Jesus said to the servants, "Fill the jars
> with water." And they filled them up to the brim. And
> he said to them, "Now draw some out and take it to the
> master of the feast." So they took it. When the master

of the feast tasted the water now become wine, and did not know where it came from (though the servants who had drawn the water knew), the master of the feast called the bridegroom and said to him, "Everyone serves the good wine first, and when people have drunk freely, then the poor wine. But you have kept the good wine until now." This, the first of his signs, Jesus did at Cana in Galilee, and manifested his glory. And his disciples believed in him. (John 2:1–11 ESV)

In the Jewish culture of Jesus's day, a wedding was an enormous celebration, not just for the couple and family, but for the entire community. Author Tim Keller wrote about this topic:

The purpose of marriage was not primarily about the happiness of the two individuals but instead to bind the community together and to raise the next generation. The purpose of marriage was the good of the commonwealth. The bigger, the stronger, and the more numerous the families of a town, the better its economy, the greater the military security, the more everyone flourished. And this meant that weddings and wedding feasts were simply a far bigger deal than they are today. The wedding feast was for the entire town because marriage was about the whole community, not merely the couple. At the same time, it was also the biggest event in the personal life of both the bride and the groom. This was the day they came of age and became full adult members of their society. It is no surprise, then, that ancient weddings went on for days—a week at least.[1]

Unfortunately, at this couple's wedding the wine ran out. In this culture, this would have been extremely embarrassing.

If uncorrected, this wine shortage would have enormous future implications for the couple and their entire family. Such a social faux pas would mean public shame and guilt for such poor planning, as well as possibly cause the loss of future deals for the family business. This was not simply, "Oops! We ran out of beverages at the party, so we'll send a guy to the convenience store for more." The ramifications of this problem might be felt in the family for generations.

Spiritually, too, there was more going on here than we might realize. For the first-century Jew, wine symbolized celebration and joy. Also, Old Testament prophets like Jeremiah[2], Hosea[3], and Amos[4] talked about the wedding and wine as a sign of the arrival of the Messiah. In addition, these same prophets talked about how the Messiah's wine would flow over the barren, dry land.

At a Jewish wedding, those celebrating were not just enjoying a fun time with the new bride and groom. They were all reminding each other of a Messiah who someday would right all the wrongs in their world.

So at this wedding in Cana, where Jesus was a guest, running out of wine was a serious matter.

Jesus's mother, Mary, came to Jesus and explained the problem to him. "They have no wine," she said, expecting that her "gifted" son could do something. His response was short and a little edgy: "Woman, what does this have to do with me? My hour has not yet come." He didn't call her Mom or Mother, but instead referred to her as "woman." He did this, I think, not to be disrespectful, but because he now was seeing the purpose of his life more clearly. His relationship with his mother was changing and would continue to change. His world-altering ministry was beginning. Soon those around him would see his true purpose for coming to earth.

So here's how this incident gives us an insight on letting go of things: Taking our hands off something inevitably means the end of something else. Not being addicted to working too much or being too busy will mean something we've been doing has to go. Letting go of hurt from someone should lead to new ways of dealing with people and how we feel when they disappoint us. What Jesus did in this moment was lift the eyes of those at the wedding to his greater purpose. They saw only that the wine jars were empty and that this was a disaster. But he showed them an uncontainable truth of the depth of his love for them. When we think of our past, our pain, our guilt, and our shame, we see only that. We struggle to move our eyes to the horizon to see the Messiah, to see our hope and the new life that he offers us.

Part of Jesus's response, though, is curious: "My hour has not yet come." In the Gospel of John, when Jesus uses the phrase "my hour," he is referring to his upcoming death on the cross. When his mother told him the party had run out of wine, Jesus answered in effect, "It is not my time to die."

I think Jesus said this because he saw, in the people dancing and cavorting at this wedding party, the brokenness of humanity—and all the guilt, shame, and regret that goes with it. He knew that the only answer to the abundant sin of people would be his death and resurrection . . . but his time hadn't come.

The apostle John, in telling this story, is conveying a symbol he doesn't want us to miss: The miracle of turning water into wine is a sign of what Jesus ultimately came to do. The shame of no more wine at the party represents the sins of the world: our sin, shame, guilt, and regret. But how would Jesus change such a grievous problem into joy?

Through purification.

Jesus told the servants to fill six stone jars with water. They weren't just any old jars—and certainly not containers normally used for storing wine. They were huge pots—each held twenty to thirty gallons—and the water they held was used for purification. As part of their religious rituals, the Jews used these jars filled with water to cleanse their body, to purify themselves before they entered into the presence of God. These rites reminded the Jews of their brokenness and sinfulness, their need for God. The act of purification also reminded them of God's holiness, how he was separate from them and that because of their sin, his people needed to be cleaned up before meeting with him.

There was something else happening here. Through his work on the cross, Jesus would provide a way to purify us, to right all the wrongs of the world. In this act of filling the purification jars and turning the water into wine, Jesus was showing us how he would do the work of purification in us.

What really happened at this wedding is that Jesus not only saved a family from a major public embarrassment . . . but he gave us a significant spiritual lesson.

But here is the big problem in our culture today: We too often don't think we need what Jesus brings. I find this is true at some level even with those of us who claim to follow Christ. We tend to think, *I'm really not in that bad a shape. I think with some time, maybe some pills and good counseling, I can fix myself.* But let me ask: Do you have anything in your life that you feel guilty about? Something you did years ago? Something you did last month? What about something that was done to you? Do you feel bitter?

What about shame? Is there abuse in your past that you can't let go of? A person you can't forgive?

How are these things to be truly repaired?

After a church service one day, a woman mentioned to me that she felt shame from her past because she'd been raped. As we talked, I asked her if she had let Jesus heal her and redeem this horrific event in her life. She said somewhat dismissively, "That's my past; I'll let it stay there."

The problem is that when we let it "stay there," it just eats at us. We cannot experience the freedom Jesus promises, the hope he brings, until we own up to our guilt, shame, and regret. And you cannot let go of something from your life until you face it, acknowledge what it has done to you, and receive the purification Jesus offers.

Your Problem and Mine

If we're honest, guilt, shame, and regret are not popular topics. They aren't positive. We don't want to be reminded of our past. We don't want to remember our guilt, shame, and regret, although we think of it often. Deep down, we know something is wrong, something is broken, but admitting it, talking about it with a spouse or counselor or even praying about it is a different story. It is hard to look up, to face what may overwhelm us. And that's why we don't feel as if we can receive the purification Jesus so abundantly offers. Sadly, we reason that if we identify with our regretful actions or thoughts, we become more like them, and that acknowledging the need for grace and forgiveness shows a weaker side of us. We think we should muster up the ability to take care of our shame or guilt. But the opposite couldn't be truer and offer more freedom.

Think for a minute: Why do you work so hard and put in all those extra hours? Why do you drive a specific car? Own a certain kind of house? Live in a certain school district? You might say, "I want my kids to have what I never had."

May I ask, "Who cares if they have what you didn't?"

"Well, I feel more worthy as a man and that I'm providing if they have what I didn't have."

May I be blunt about some of these issues? Here are some things that I think we should ask anytime we feel so tied to material things and what others think of us. All of our trying to impress and perhaps even make up for something that has happened in our lives should be run through these filters:

- Why is the opinion of others so important? Why is what your spouse thinks about you so important? Why does it matter if your parents think you are worthwhile?
- Why do you need to be right all the time? When was the last time you said, "I'm wrong. I'm sorry." If you can't remember, that's a red flag.
- Why do you worry so much about how you look? What is it about your body that makes you struggle to believe

God planned every inch of it for his glory? Why do you feel the need to compare yourself to a woman or man on an airbrushed magazine cover?

- Why do you insist on being independent and not needing anyone around? Why can't you ask for help?
- Why are you so dependent on other people? Why can't you go anywhere alone?
- If you don't complete your to-do list and there are things on it at the end of the day, why do you feel like a failure?
- If you get passed over for a promotion, will you feel crushed? Why?

Based on my own experiences and struggles in these areas, I believe that you are thinking this way and doing things because there is something wrong (you aren't wrong, but there is something in you that is showing up), and you may be trying to prove yourself or fix yourself to cover up what is broken. You want to numb the pain by cleansing yourself of the shame and guilt. But we all know that this is only temporary before the dam breaks inside each of us and we are forced to address what we know is there and has been festering inside of us before it severely affects our lives and our family. And this is the direction I was headed in before I took a serious look at why I was doing so much in my life—none of it very fulfilling for me at the time.

I have some very good news for you. Someone has already provided for your healing from brokenness and now offers you the opportunity to truly let go of your past. But we need to fully acknowledge and allow it to change who we are—inside and out.

Knowing the Real You

If you're like most people, this sounds too good to be true. We often see a vision of the person we want to become, but wonder if it's really possible. For us. "Can I really let go of what I've carried for the last fifteen years? Can I really let go of always having to be right and spending energy trying to prove myself? Can I really begin trusting people and be a part of life-giving community? Can I really stop making myself pay for something that Jesus has already forgiven me for?"

Yes.

So I ask you in the spirit of taking a look at what's inside of you: What makes you YOU? What does your true self look like?

Did you notice in the earlier example of the wedding that Jesus didn't change the situation that led to this couple running out of wine? For this family, I believe that the miracle that Jesus did for them is what defined them—not the fact that they ran out of wine. The memory of this near disaster would remain. He did, however, change their present and their future. That's exactly what Jesus wants to do for all of us—*now*!

The regret you have about your past, those you have hurt, the things you have done, you will always have those memories. They are forever a part of your story. Letting go does not mean they will magically disappear or cease to be true. But the memories from the past don't have to suffocate you so that you can't move forward and become who Jesus created you to be. The shame you carry about what was done to you, the memories of abuse, the way you feel in the pit of your stomach at the thought of that person and what happened, is a part of your story. But it's not the end of the story!

Without realizing it, you can let your guilt, shame, and regret define you. Your past becomes more than a part of you—it becomes you. But these things don't reflect the true you. It's a small part of a larger story in process with who you are and where you are going. You may say these things to yourself over and over:

"I'm an addict."

"I'm the guy who got his girlfriend pregnant."

"I'm the girl who can't be alone."

"I'm the guy who can't stop working."

"I'm the girl who counts calories."

"I'm the guy who fears not mattering."

When we trap ourselves like this, we reveal that we do not understand God's grace. It's easy to think God's grace, forgiveness, and life transformation are for other people, especially if you walk around with guilt, shame, and regret. Or maybe you continue to live in hurt and sin, longing for freedom from an addiction or a temptation, because you are not able to find or stick to a plan to conquer it once and for all.

The apostle John closes his story of the wedding miracle by telling us that through this sign and many others, Jesus's glory was seen and his disciples believed in him (John 2:11). In a symbolic way, through this one miraculous event, Jesus announced that he was the Messiah, the one who was able to take care of our guilt, shame, and regret—to purify us of our insidious sin.

Tim Keller also wrote,

Jesus, the king, created all things in love. He has the power and the beauty to see His vision for the world through to its glorious end; to undo everything we have been able to do to harm it. To accomplish that, He had to come and die for it. Three days later, He rose again; and one day will come back again to usher in a renewed creation. The gospel is the ultimate story that shows victory coming out of defeat, strength coming out of weakness, life coming out of death, rescue from abandonment. And because it is a true story, it gives us hope because we know that life is really like that. It can be your story as well. God made you to love Him supremely, but He lost you. He returned to get you back, but it took the cross to do it. He absorbed your darkness so that one day you can finally and dazzlingly become your true self and take your seat at His eternal feast.[5]

I urge you this very moment to receive the miracle Jesus has for you—to have him perform the purification of your sin and give you the freedom and power to be the real, true you.

And then, with new confidence, let go of your past.

Take a moment and think what this would look like in your life. Not just right now and tomorrow, but five years from now. The heartbreak you've carried since you were a child that has defined you, what would your life be like without that? The way you have made your spouse or kids pay for what was done to you, how would your relationship change if you stopped making them pay for someone else's actions? What kind of joy could enter that relationship?

What if you stopped working the way you do, stopped trying to gain the approval of a spouse, boss, or parent? Think of the freedom that comes from believing that *because of Jesus's work on the cross and his resurrection, I am approved. Nothing I do can make me more loved, more forgiven, more accepted than I am right now.*

This is the truth of how Jesus changes our water into wine and moves our lives forward so we can experience the life he created us to live.

Breathing New Air

Although Jesus has accomplished the act of purification, the actual complete working out of this cleansing is a process that takes time for most people. You've probably carried around your guilt, shame, and regret for years. Becoming comfortable in your new life will take some reminders. Daily, we need to identify the lies we may still be tempted to believe, the shame that creeps in, the regrets we carry. All of that needs exposure to the purifying light of the truth that Jesus brings.

As mentioned in Chapter Six, Tim Chester lists four gospel truths that battle the lies of control, power, approval, and comfort that we have discussed. Here's his list again:

1. God is great—so we don't have to be in control (control).
2. God is glorious—so we don't have to fear others (approval).
3. God is good—so we don't have to look elsewhere (comfort).

4. God is gracious—so we don't have to prove ourselves (power).[6]

One of the things I've done is to memorize these simple phrases. When I feel past guilt creeping up, when I start believing the old lies, I simply repeat these phrases.

For a while on my journey, I made these four phrases the opening screen when I turned on my computer. You might want to try the same exercise—or post the phrases on your bathroom mirror—until you no longer need to be reminded that with Jesus, the power of the past is broken.

Discussion Questions

1. What is the root of the guilt, shame, or regret in your life?

2. What do you wish you could change about your past? Why do you have a hard time letting go of that?

3. Read John 2:1–11 and the story of the wedding we looked at in the chapter. How has Jesus purified you through his life, death, and resurrection?

4. If you are purified in Jesus, what would it look like to let go of your past, guilt, shame, and regret?

Chapter 9

When Your Past Won't Stay in the Past

Memories are powerful. I am always amazed at the things I remember . . . and forget. Smells, sights, sounds—all of these provoke memories for us.

The other day I heard a song that made me think back to eighth grade and my trying to work up the courage to ask a girl to join me for a couples skate at the roller rink. As that memory awakened, all I could think about was how awkward I had felt, the pain when she said no, and how in my eighth grade mind my life was over.

Other memories are happier but equally powerful. You might smell apple pie or another favorite food and remember a grandparent you were close to. You can taste something and remember a trip to Europe or an anniversary dinner you never want to forget.

These experiences are why pictures and keepsakes are so important too. They represent memories we don't want to forget, reminders of events we treasured, places we've visited, or people we have enjoyed.

Pleasant memories make us feel warm on the inside, but bad memories tie us in knots. These are the memories we would like to forget, but then a trigger awakens all the pain. You see a house, hear a song, enter a room, and the images of abuse, hurt, heartache, and pain come like a flash flood. In a split second you are back in a moment or series of events that forever changed your life, or at least significantly altered your view of love, marriage, acceptance, or worth. Often these memories are particularly painful—not because of things we did, but because of things done to us. A parent who abandoned us. A relative who abused us. A spouse who cheated on us, then left. A rebellious child who said incredibly hurtful words. A teacher who continually put us down. A boss who lied and denied us the raise or promotion.

Some of our painful memories are moments that we created, foolish times when we lacked judgment or didn't listen to parents or friends and found ourselves in a mess—like a destructive relationship. Or maybe we chased dreams that were not meant to be.

As the end of this book nears and, I hope, you now see how breathing room is not only possible but can definitely be a reality in your life, I want to issue a warning of sorts. The possibilities of a new way to live are exciting. Letting go of habits and addictions, walking away from hurtful memories, seeing how to have a schedule that brings peace, sanity, and joy—all of this is energizing.

So why the warning?

It is tempting to think that life will be smooth sailing from this point forward. In some ways, it will be. But in other ways, it will be difficult. One thing I've learned about the past: memories always come back. You will always be from the same family of origin and from the place where you grew up. You are always connected to the experiences you have walked through. The people who have hurt you the most are often still in your life.

Many books, and even some pastors in their sermons, have oversold the idea that we can be completely free from our past. To some extent that is true, but in other ways it is impossible.

Yes, you should curtail relationships with destructive and abusive people. But sometimes those people are your parents or an ex-spouse. So what do you do when you bump into them at a wedding, funeral, or family reunion? Sometimes you will have to walk back into their life or they will walk back into yours.

Yes, because of the power of Jesus, you can be *free* from the bondage of your past. Those hurtful memories don't need to take up space in your heart. But what do you do with the practical reality when a person who harmed you reenters your life, even for a few minutes?

You Are Not Alone

The Gospel of John is one of my favorite Bible books. I particularly like it because, unlike the other three Gospels, it creates more images of Jesus than the others—the material is more symbolic. The writer's goal is the same as the other Gospels in that John wants us to know who Jesus is, what Jesus has done, what Jesus is doing—so that we can believe and have life (see John 20:30–31). But elsewhere in the book, in chapters 13–17, John relates how Jesus prepares his disciples to live on earth without him physically being with them, because he must return to heaven. This section of the book is by far my favorite, because it is written not just to the disciples who were with Jesus, but also directly to us! Jesus is telling us what to expect, too, because he won't be with us physically.

Jesus's disciples have spent three years with him, hearing him teach and watching him perform miracles. They have seen lame people walk, blind people see, deaf people hear. He has fed five thousand people from one person's lunch, and raised people from the dead. Jesus and "the guys" have had meals together, camped out, and shared long conversations about the meaning of life and what the future will hold.

Then we read in John 13 how the disciples learn that his time with them is coming to an end; he won't always be with them. At first this news jars them. So Jesus sets about trying to comfort them. He tells them that he is the way, the truth, and the life, and that no one comes to the Father except through him (John 14:6). He also says that he is going to the Father to prepare a place for his followers and that he will come back for them (John 14:3).

Then he tells them that if they will believe in him and follow his commandments, their lives will matter and they will accomplish greater works than he did (John 14:12). What an incredible statement! Jesus has raised people from the dead, healed people who couldn't walk, see, or hear. Would the disciples really be able to do these and even greater things? (In fact, as the New Testament reveals, they did end up doing all these things.)

As if this isn't enough, Jesus tells them that after his death, resurrection, and ascension, he will send a Helper (John 14:16). The word for Helper carries the idea of someone who is similar but different. And so it is—the Helper that Jesus sent, the Holy Spirit, lives in the followers of Jesus, not physically walking next to them as Jesus did with his first disciples, but in the hearts of those who choose to accept the teachings and ways of Jesus. It is a powerful thought, and often we minimize it or live as if this important truth doesn't exist.

Pruning

And there's still more.

Jesus then tells the disciples that he is the true vine. God the Father is the farmer, and the Father prunes the branches, which are the followers of Jesus (John 15:1–2). The point of pruning is to allow good fruit to grow. The farmer knows exactly what the branches need and when pruning will help them produce good fruit. The vine has no clue.

Pruning is not easy or comfortable work. It involves cutting off branches, which means something about our lives will change. What we may not understand, though, is how close Jesus and the Father are to us in the pruning process. In fact, the moments when God feels the furthest from us are the times he is the closest to us. Let me explain.

Jesus tells his followers that they need to abide in or stay close to him (John 15:4). This is the key to living in the freedom of Jesus; this is also the key to breathing room. What Jesus meant is that

God allows and sends things into our lives to help us become the people he has designed us to be. These things help us become more like what he had in mind way back when he created us. So the moments of pruning (the connotation we think about is cutting back or having something cut out in some way or shape from our lives), though they may seem very unpleasant, are when God is preparing us for something more, something better (John 15:11).

So, when it feels like God is far away, in fact he is close!

Remember the image of the vine and the farmer. Pruning does not often have the goal we have for our lives. Our goal for pruning is that it would make us thinner, richer, better parents, or enable us to have a better job. The pruning Jesus brings is to help us bear more fruit—fruit that lasts (John 15:2). That fruit, we are told in Galatians, is love, joy, peace, patience, kindness, goodness, faithfulness, gentleness, and self-control (Gal. 5:22–23).

We aren't to have just one of these or a few of these. We are to see all that fruit in our lives. A follower of Jesus is not able to say, "I'm just not a patient guy," or "I don't have self-control." No, followers of Jesus should have all these qualities and see these fruits growing in their lives.

God brings this fruit into our lives through pruning, through giving us opportunities to grow. Here's an example.

Most people I know aren't very patient. We want things immediately: food, status updates, car rides, everything. We even post our pictures on Instagram, which reveals this desire for speed. But if we need to grow in patience, God will not just give it to us. He will give us opportunities to learn patience.

I think this is often why memories—or situations that act as triggers—from our past come flooding back to us, often at times we don't want them to. God may bring a difficult person into your life so that you will grow by having an opportunity to learn how to love someone you don't naturally love because of how that person has treated you. Or he may have you unexpectedly encounter the person who wronged you. Just remember, God is the farmer; he knows what needs to happen for you to bear fruit that will carry you well into your years ahead so that you can withstand all that comes at you in this world—not just your past, but your future.

James, the brother of Jesus, saw this. Think for a minute about the change in James' life. We are told in the Gospels that the siblings of Jesus thought he was crazy, yet by the time Acts 15 rolls around, James is the leader of the largest New Testament church. In his short book, James tells us the goal of adversity and pain: "that you may be perfect and complete, lacking in nothing" (James 1:4 ESV).

In my darker moments I've often wondered why God has allowed certain things to happen. The years 2005–2007 were by far the hardest of my life. Katie and I learned she was pregnant with our first child, which was incredibly exciting, except that four months into the pregnancy, I unexpectedly lost my job. Like most twenty-five-year-olds, I was convinced that it was "them" and not me. So we packed up and moved from Baltimore to Wisconsin. Less than eight months after moving to Wisconsin, I lost another job. Again, it was them, not me.

At this point, almost out of breath, I wasn't sure what to do. It was that moment that we all encounter, that moment that decides if we move forward with breathing room or if we continue to live in a way that suffocates us.

Then sunlight broke through. I got a job as a student pastor in Colorado. We packed up and got ready to move. After I drove to Colorado with a car full of stuff, I met with the new pastor I was going to be working for and he said, "Josh, after talking about it, we're pulling back our job offer."

The drive from Colorado back to Kansas City (where we were living) was the longest ten hours of my life. God and I had it out. After I got back and told Katie what had happened, as we sat on the couch in the darkness, she looked at me and said, "When are you going to learn whatever it is God is trying to teach you so we can move forward?"

This moment is crucial in our lives. We often miss the chance to move forward, not because we can't wait to get to the future, but because we haven't fully dealt with our past.

Dealing with our past is pruning, and pruning is painful. The moment of pruning, and how we respond, determines if we are able to move forward into the future God has for us.

When Adversity Hits

Jesus told us that our lives here on earth would not be trouble-free . . . but that he had overcome the troubles we face (see John 16:33). In John 14 and 15 Jesus was encouraging his followers to give them hope for what life would be like after he left. But he didn't simply give them an inspiring pep talk: he brought reality to the conversation. He told them life would be hard.

In John 15:18 he said they would be hated by the world. Jesus wasn't just talking about a culture opposed to Christian beliefs. That was included—the world that can be seen. But he was also talking about what can't be seen, the world of Satan and the demons that fight against us.

Adversity is so tough because most of the time we have no warning when it will hit. We don't know when we will lose a job, when a spouse will walk out, when we won't get a promotion, when a child will walk away from us, or when a relative will die.

This recently happened in our neighborhood to a family who attends our church. The wife was having stomach pain and went for medical tests. The doctor told her, "You have pancreatic cancer, and it is in your liver and lymph nodes. You only have months to live." As we sat with this family, they were in utter shock and disbelief. Imagine thinking you are a basically healthy person, and then some tests reveal that you have cancer.

Obviously, we have little control over what will happen in life, so we need to be spiritually prepared for adversity. Tim Keller has said, "Nothing is more important than to learn how to maintain a life of purpose in the midst of painful adversity."[1] However, as Americans, and even as Christians, we often seem unprepared to handle adversity.

Remember . . .

In John 15 and 16, after telling his disciples that they will face adversity and that finishing life will be hard, Jesus uses a word that is easy to miss in the passage: "Remember," he says. In fact, he as good as tells them, "I've said these things—talking about heaven, the afterlife, coming back for my followers, sending the Helper, doing greater works, pruning, abiding, and even facing adversity—so that when it happens, you won't fall away" (John

16:1). So that "when their hour comes you may *remember* that I told them to you" (John 16:4 ESV, emphasis mine).

Remembering is not always easy to do—especially in the middle of a crisis. It is easy to forget the good times when life gets tough. When your life is hard, it is easy to be envious of the life someone else has. It is easy to forget how God has provided in the past when you are up against present bills you can't pay. It is easy to forget how God got you into a program or school when you fail to make an internship or fail to make the dean's list. It is easy to forget how God provided you with a spouse when that spouse is difficult to live with. It is easy to forget the blessing of your child when he is screaming at 2 A.M. or difficult to connect with as a teenager. It is easy to forget that God provides a way out of temptation when you fail and fall back into old patterns.

When all that happens, Jesus says to *remember* what he has said and what he has done.

How do we remember, though? How do we walk through adversity? How do we face our past and win?

With help. We have been given an incredible, always available, 24/7, live-in Helper in the Holy Spirit. Jesus told his disciples, "I will not leave you as orphans. I will come to you. I will send you the Helper" (John 14:16, 18, my paraphrase). As a follower of Jesus, you do not face your past alone; you don't face that temptation or question alone. You do not face your calendar or those choices by yourself. You don't face your finances or body image by yourself. *You never have to face anything alone!*

The word *orphan* is an interesting one for Jesus to use. In the first century, orphans were helpless and destitute. There was no system to help them—no humanitarian agencies—and families were not adopting the way they are today. Orphans needed help to survive. However, I think there is more to this than just being lost, hopeless, and destitute. Children did not become orphans without something painful or horrible happening. Parents had to give them up or abandon them.

As we know even today, some parents don't care about their children and will abandon them. But other parents are not able to provide for their kids, and through their tears place their children up for adoption. Katie and I have adopted two boys, so we know firsthand how the pain looks in the faces of parents as they place their kids for adoption. There is also adversity for the adopting family. A child does not become part of a family without stress. If the kids are older, they bring added baggage and pain. If they are from a different country, there are barriers of both language and culture.

Adoption is great when it comes to our past. According to Ephesians 1, the moment we begin following Jesus, we are adopted into a new family, a new way of life. We are given a new story. Our past is replaced by our future with Jesus.

This picture has become a reality for our family as we've adopted two boys, one domestically and one from Ethiopia. Naïvely, I saw adopting a child as simply adding one to your family, much like having a baby. It is similar, but entirely different.

While these boys have a new future because of their adoption, their past is still a part of their journey and our lives. They have a new identity, a new name, a new opportunity to succeed, but their past is still there. Sometimes it interacts with their present, but it never ceases to be a part of their journey.

In the moments of doubt, failure, pain, and adversity, Jesus tells us to not be surprised by those times. Instead, we are to face them with courage, because he warned us they were coming. And in those moments we are to remember what he has done and that we are not alone. We are not orphans. This is part of God's plan to help us move closer to who he created us to become.

Rest in Jesus

After that time in Colorado where I was told I did not have a job as a youth pastor, with my car still full of our stuff, I drove home and on the way had the most honest (and loudest) conversation with God I've ever had. I was angry, hurt, disillusioned, and wondering why God had sold me out. Here I was trying to serve him, and he was making it hard. This is how the journey to freedom can often feel as we think, *I'm just trying to get free. Why can't it be easier?*

As I lay in bed that night and over the coming days, I wrestled with that question: "What is God trying to teach me?"

If I'm honest with you, the struggles and pain I walked through during those two hard years were not just because of the pastors I had worked for. It was me. It was my desire to be great, my desire to be in charge, the pride that pushed me. And I was also struggling to trust others and submit to leadership.

I was learning that *the moment of adversity is also the moment of faith*—of stepping out and believing not just in ourselves but in our God.

Our faith is not in some idea, but in a person. A person we can trust. A person who has conquered all things, including our sin, death, and Satan. There is no one who would rather us dwell on our past than our enemy. But there is nothing that can stand against us because of what Jesus has done and who Jesus is.

That is what we rest in. It is what I rested in during that season and in coming seasons of church planting, adding kids to our family, and dealing with my past. It is what you can rest in, too, as you move forward and let go of your past.

Even when your past comes back, it doesn't have to affect your future.

Breathing New Air

Take a few minutes before we move on to the final chapter to take an inventory of where you think your heart is right now. Please don't skip this opportunity to evaluate how persistent memories from the past are keeping you from growing into greater freedom and strength in Christ.

Which fruits of the spirit is God trying to grow in you right now? Love, joy, peace, patience, kindness, goodness, faithfulness, gentleness, or self-control?

Take a moment to thank God for the forgiveness you have received in your own life. Think about what it means that your sins are forgiven, that your past has been paid for through the death and resurrection of Jesus.

Take a moment to pray for and think about the people who need your forgiveness, the people who have hurt you the most, the ones who have taken up residence in your heart and mind.

What are you facing in your life that seems impossible, insurmountable? You are not an orphan. The Helper is with you. Breathe deeply! Take courage!

Discussion Questions

1. Why is it so easy for our past to come back to haunt us and remind us of things we'd like to forget?

2. Why is it so hard to forgive and forget things?

3. Why do you have a hard time forgiving yourself for things you've done?

4. How does abiding in Jesus change your view of your past as you move into your future?

5. How does abiding and resting in Jesus allow you to enter your unknown future with confidence?

Chapter 10

Breathing New Air
(Living on Purpose)

Meaning is one of those words that gets used a lot in our culture. We talk about purpose, read books about figuring out our purpose in life, and struggle with wondering what to do with our lives after high school and college. Then, when we get married, we struggle to understand how that has changed things and what we should do with our lives now.

I recently turned thirty-five, and women told Katie to beware of the midlife crisis that was apparently waiting for us on the other side of thirty-five. For many men, this is a time when they look at their lives and dislike how they have turned out. They look back, wondering what they gave their lives to. Many men struggle with the amount of time they spent away from home working, wondering if they built anything of worth. They wonder if they have amassed the wealth they should have, or if they will be remembered for anything. For many men, this stems from what we talked about in Chapter Seven and the father wound—that wound that reminds you of the withheld affection and approval of your father, the high standard he set for you, or the embarrassment that he was to you, so you've worked to not be that way.

For women, this struggle of meaning is similar, but different. Women struggle as their identity switches from a wife, a working wife, a stay-at-home mom, a working mom, empty nester, and a combination of those. Magazines are littered with headlines about how to have the perfect beach body in six weeks, how to have the hottest mind-blowing sex with your husband, and how to avoid wrinkles and unwanted gray hair. TV shows show you how to have the spotless house, and how to fix things up so that they are trendy but still artsy.

As I talk with men and women about breathing room, one thing continues to come up: "If I slow down, if I do what you are saying, I'm not sure what I'll do in the silence." For many, the idea of breathing room is scarier than working too much and having a heart attack.

Why Meaning Matters

I've waited until now to talk about meaning. If you remember our fictitious family in Chapter Two, the one running from one thing to the next, you'll remember the struggle that the father had about accomplishments and the longing to feel that his life was leading somewhere or was worthwhile.

This is common among those who lack breathing room. In our effort to stay busy, when we stop to think about why we are doing what we're doing, if it is sustainable or even worthwhile, we will begin to wonder about our purpose in life. One of the lessons I've learned is that without a clearly defined purpose for your life and the life of your family, you will always struggle with breathing room and relationships.

How We Miss Breathing Room in Our Search for Meaning

When you have a clearly defined purpose in life, other things fall into place.

If you think about your job, there is a budget. Your family has a budget too. For most families, as we saw in Chapter Three, the struggle of money sucks breathing room right out of our lives. When members of a company know why they exist, what their purpose is, what they are trying to accomplish, then they know where money should go, what they should give their time to, and what priorities should be most important. The same is true for families.

Most people, most families simply spend money on the things in front of them. They sign up their kids for the same activities that others are signing their kids up for without ever asking, "Is this the right thing for us to do right now?"

In the end, if meaning and purpose are not clearly defined, everything is a good idea. Everything is worth doing. Why? Because we've never clarified the win.

This is a simple leadership idea. Whenever you see a company, church, or family that is effective, you will see people who have clarified the "win." You will also see people who have clarified the "loss." This is where most people stop. We like the idea of clarifying the win, finding our purpose, but are often unwilling to clarify the loss and stick to it. The reason is that we fear missing out, or we fear that someone will get mad. What happens if you clarify the win for your family and it means that your wife quits her job? What if the win means you quit the elder team or the PTA? What happens if in clarifying the win, your son will play less baseball this coming year? You will buy less to get a handle on your finances instead of them handling you?

Now, all those wins are things you long for: living at a sustainable pace, creating a schedule that is maintainable, having a bank account that isn't wildly out of control, erasing debt, and spending more time with your kids and influencing their lives instead of the day-care workers doing so. All good things. But the loss can be overwhelming. The loss is what hurts. The loss and the fear of how that loss will feel is what stops us in this search for meaning, and consequently, it is the last and most important thing that keeps us from breathing room.

A Hidden Misery

You might be thinking, as most people do, "But everyone I know seems so happy and well adjusted as they run up a mountain of debt, run from one thing to the next, sign their kids up for three summer camps, overlap sports teams, do four bake sales in a two-week time span, and attend church four nights a week."

In reality, all those people you know are just as unhappy and lost as you are. They aren't sure why they are doing anything, only that everyone else seems to be doing the same thing. They aren't sure why they are on earth or what their goal is, only that they are taking up space. They aren't sure what to do with their past hurts, and maybe like you've tried to do while reading this book, they tried to let go of them—and while some hurts have gone away, others still come back to haunt them.

Systems Trump Hopes and Intentions

While I was getting my master's in organizational leadership, I remember hearing a professor quote W. Edwards Deming. Deming was trained as a mathematical physicist. He helped develop the sampling techniques still used by the U.S. Census Bureau and the Bureau of Labor Statistics. He also helped to rebuild Japan after World War II and helped them understand how to be more effective as a country and in their industries. In fact, Deming is credited as the inspiration for what became known as the Japanese postwar economic miracle of 1950 to 1960, when Japan rose from the ashes of war to become the second most powerful economy in the world in less than a decade.[1]

He was famous for many sayings, but one has always stuck out to me: *Your system is perfectly designed to give you the results you are getting.* Read that again: *Your system is perfectly designed to give you the results you are getting.* This means how you feel is actually how you should feel right now based on the system you have. Your finances and schedule are exactly where they should be, based on the system you have in place. How you've dealt with past hurts, past addictions, and sins has left you exactly where you should be based on the system you have.

In our culture, though, we don't live as if this is true. We live on hopes and intentions.

That's what New Year's resolutions are. This is the year I'm going to lose weight, get out of debt, slow down, read more, play with my kids more, spend more time with friends, look for a new job, or take a class. All hopes. All intentions. Yet, as we've seen, most people don't keep their good intentions called New Year's resolutions for more than a week, let alone a quarter of the year or the whole year.

Why?

They don't have a system set up for it. They don't have a way to turn their hopes and intentions into a way of life.

It is the same way with breathing room. If you don't have a system for it, breathing room will be another book you read that you never apply; it will simply be a hope or a good intention.

Let's put Deming's words another way: *Systems trump hopes and intentions.*

Nothing just happens, and that's what hopes and intentions are—thinking things will just happen.

Before we lay out a system that can turn your hopes and intentions into reality, let's look at some of your hopes and good intentions. A year from now, what do you hope will be true about your life? If you have kids, what do you want to see them accomplish in the next year? Do you hope something will be different in your marriage? In your finances or career? Think about some of the hopes and intentions you have. Now, do you have a system for them to become a reality?

If you are like most people, the answer to this is no.

Discovering a System

One of the questions I get a lot as a pastor centers on God's will. For many Christians, it is a mystery. What does God want me to do with my life? Who does God want me to marry? What happens if I marry the wrong person? What if I go to the wrong college? Take the wrong job? End up in the wrong career? For many, these questions are paralyzing.

I don't think figuring out God's will is as mysterious as we make it out to be. In fact, I think God's will is all over the Bible.

When it comes to God's will and making decisions, Katie and I have stayed away from listing the pros and cons. You've seen this. You are facing a choice, and so the rational part of our brains asks, "Which way is better?" So we list the pros and cons, what we will gain and what we will lose depending on which way we go. Never once does purpose, breathing room, long-term happiness, or short-term pain enter the conversation. I think this is a wrong way to go about finding God's will and making decisions.

Instead, ask this question: *Will this opportunity get me to where I believe God is leading, or will it hinder me?*[2]

I find this does a couple of things. First, it takes the pressure off of this particular decision you are facing. It broadens the horizon of what you are thinking about and trying to figure out. It is no longer about what I do next, but what I do ultimately. Second, it lifts your eyes up from what you are facing so that you see the need for a larger picture and a better system. By seeing this way, I believe you are able to see as God sees, which is the larger picture. And let's be honest, our stress goes down when we are past something and we see things more clearly.

But I Don't Know . . .

Often, when I lay out this idea to people, they will respond with what you might be thinking. "What if I don't know my purpose? What if I don't have any meaning? What if I don't know where God is leading me, so I don't know if this opportunity helps to propel me to that preferred future or hinders me? What do I do then?"

First, the biblical perspective on things.

I said earlier that I think we make God's will more mysterious and mystical than it actually is. If you read through Scripture, you see that God wants us to glorify and enjoy him. That we are to reflect God to those around us. We looked at this in Chapter Four when we talked about reflecting the image of God to the world around us.

How about marriage? God has told us in Ephesians 5 and Genesis 1–2 that there are specific roles for marriage. Men are to lovingly lead their wives and families. They are to pastor them. They are to lay down their lives as Jesus did. They are to exhibit servant leadership. They have been given responsibility and accountability by God for their families. Wives are to respond to their husbands' leadership and submit to them. They are to be their partners in life, their helpers, giving pushback when needed. This doesn't mean a wife is a robot or a doormat. The Holy Spirit is called "the Helper," so I don't think this is a negative thing as we speak of it.

Take money, as we looked at in Chapter Three. We are told in Malachi 3 and 2 Corinthians 8–9 that we are to be good stewards of the money and possessions God entrusts to us. We are to honor God by giving back to him a portion of what he has entrusted to us. That portion is to be sacrificial, generous, worshipful, and proportional. This means we need to set this aside first and then live within our means on what is left.

Work and rest? We are to live in rhythm. If we are married, 1 Timothy 5 says that a man is responsible to provide for his family; that if he doesn't, he is worse than an unbeliever. This means we need to live within our means. Titus 2 says that younger moms with small kids are not to find their identity in their jobs and careers but in the role God has given them as a wife and a mom. It doesn't say it is wrong for a woman to work, but it does say her identity is not to be found in that. A simple question: "Are you more known as a woman for what you do for a living or for being a wife and a mom?" The answer to that question shows your identity.

And finally, living on mission and discipleship. We are told in Matthew 28, Acts 1, and scores of other places that we are to live on mission. That the gospel should change us in such a way that we live our lives with the purpose of moving the gospel forward in the world in which we live. That we should live lives that are different. If you live out the passages mentioned above, do you think your life will look different from those around you?

While these are broad lines, they are also very specific. You can glorify God and accomplish what he calls you to by doing any number of things. But we often think wrongly about this because we want the one thing God has for us. I've heard well-meaning pastors say to those considering becoming pastors, "If you can see yourself doing anything else, go and do that." On the one hand, there is truth in this, because being a pastor is hard work. Being a doctor, a business owner, mechanic, artist, or stay-at-home mom is equally hard, just in different ways. The reason this is bad advice is that if you have any talent whatsoever, there are a number of things you could do and enjoy. I could own and enjoy owning a CrossFit box or being a personal trainer, but that isn't the best way for me to glorify God and disciple people. While I was in college, I thought about being a lawyer. The idea of getting paid to argue seemed so irresistible to me, but that isn't the best way for me to glorify God and disciple people. The best way for me to glorify God and use the gifts he's given to me is by pastoring a church and developing other leaders to plant more churches.

Also, the practical side begins to enter this conversation. How do you figure out what you can do to best glorify and enjoy God, to reflect him to the world around you, and to make disciples? In his book *Catalyst Leader*,[3] Brad Lomenick lists some incredibly helpful questions:

- What are your passions and gifts? At the intersection of these two elements, you'll find your purpose in life.
- What would you work on or want to do for free? That is usually a good sign of what God has designed you to do.
- What energized you when you were a child? Does it still animate you? Knowing your calling is often directly connected to childhood passions and gifts.
- If you could do anything and take a pay cut, what would that be? You may have to blow up your financial goals in order to pursue your true calling.
- What barriers are preventing you from pursuing your true calling? Can you begin removing those?
- If you aren't engaging your gifts and talents where you find yourself now, could you make changes in your

current role to better engage those? Don't rule out the possibility that where you are is where you need to be.

If this is an area you are struggling with, I would encourage you to take some time and think through your answers to these questions. Talk through them with your spouse or a close friend. If you struggle to figure something out, ask for help. Oftentimes, those who spend time with us know us better than we know ourselves and know what makes us light up with passion.

In looking at these questions, let me point out a couple of things. First, the question on what you would do for free is one I often ask people who are struggling with direction. The answer to that question reveals a lot about us. There are lots of things we would do for money, but not a lot we would do for free. Many times, as you consider your gifts, passions, what fired you up as a child, and what you would do for free, you will begin to find a dream you have always thought about. Maybe it's starting a business, being more artistic, going overseas to help those with less, or working less to volunteer more. Often your passions can be seen in the things you complain about. Do you look at your church, business, or the world around you and say, "Why isn't anybody doing ____?" That's your passion.

I started Revolution Church because statistically, 20- to 40-year-old men are those least likely to attend church on a given week in this country. Females are 70 percent of church attendees in the United States. In the city I live in, Tucson, less than 7 percent of the city attends church twice a month, and we are less churched than Seattle and Las Vegas. I looked at the landscape of churches and said, "Why isn't anyone doing more to reach men?" My passion is wrapped up in the reality that most of our culture's problems stem from a father wound, from men not fulfilling what God has called them to be. If you look at prisons, problems in relationships, workaholism, stress, and addictions, the failure of men is one of the main root problems. We started Revolution because I couldn't stop thinking about that issue, and no one else seemed to be doing anything about it in Tucson. People cared, people agreed that it was an issue, but they didn't have a burning passion for it like I wanted them to have.

As I walked down that road, I began to see how I am wired to lead. From the time I was a child, I put things together. I thought up ideas, was creative, and had visions of what could be. Whenever I was in a group setting in school, work, or church, I took charge of it. I never waited to see who would step up and make something happen; I made it happen. When we started Revolution, I took a 70 percent pay cut to start the church. I almost worked for free. But it was worth it.

The In-Between

If you look at that list of questions again, you may realize how the last one applies to your life. You may be in the exact spot that God wants you to be in. This could be tough for you to hear.

We don't talk a lot about this in any circle of life, because much of life is how we can move on to the next stage of life, take the next step in our career, or advance in some way. Many times, we are exactly where God wants us to be.

Let's say that is you. You want to move forward into something else, something that fits your passion, but nothing seems to open up. You've tried to make changes to start a business, or maybe you've started one and have failed. You've tried to take classes, and nothing has happened. What do you do?

This is what is called the desert.

This is the time of waiting, a time of preparation. If you look at the life of any leader in the Bible—Moses, David, Daniel, Nehemiah, Jesus, and Paul—they all went through a time of waiting and preparation. Some lasted forty years, like Moses. Some lasted forty days, like Jesus. Some involved prison and capture, like Joseph, Daniel, and Paul. David went on the run for his life. Nehemiah had to deal with critics who tried to keep him from fulfilling what God called him to do.

Just because things aren't coming together for you on your timetable, in the way that you want, does not mean you are on the wrong path or that you misheard God. It may take longer.

When I was twenty-one, I felt God was calling me to plant a church. I didn't plant it until I was twenty-nine, and I did it in a city I had never been to before. So many times, what seems so clear to us and is from God, doesn't happen on our timetable. If you think about it, this is one reason many people lose breathing room in their lives. They try to take control of the things only God has control of, such as time. In an effort to move things along, to move things to the place we think God wants them to be (and we want them to be), we try to take control of things we shouldn't and we end up losing life instead of gaining it.

Defining Your Family's Purpose

If you are a parent, one of your jobs is to lay out the goal and purpose of your family. As already mentioned, if you don't do this, disaster is just waiting to strike. Without knowing why your family exists, the values you want to live out, the kind of adults you want your kids to be, anything is a good idea and anything is worth doing or spending your money on.

Sadly, this is something few parents actually think through.

It is easy to get caught up in the day-to-day work of parenting. Car rides, practices, recitals, homework, and other activities take our attention and time. We never step back to ask, "Is what we are doing as a family going to get our family and our kids where we want them to be? Where we believe God wants us to be?"

So let's take a step back and think about breathing room from a purposeful family perspective.

When we think about purpose and meaning in our lives, what things we pass on to our kids, I think it is important to start with the end in mind. As you think about your life, your family, your kids, what they will know when they leave your house, what people will think of your family, the reputation you will have as a family, what people will know about your family, what are those things? Often people will talk about what things will be said at someone's funeral as a litmus test for this.

As a pastor, I do a number of funerals. It is amazing what things people say at funerals. I remember one in particular, a funeral for a man in his sixties. I didn't know him very well, but his adult kids attended my church and they asked if I would do the funeral. I went to spend some time with the family to hear stories of the man and pastor them through this moment. When I got there, it wasn't a scene of weeping, but of silence. After meeting everyone, I said, "So, tell me about Jim.[4] What things do you remember that made you laugh or what fond memories do you have from being kids?"

Silence.

So I waited.

Finally, one of the sons said, "He sure liked salsa."

What stuck in my mind about this moment was that Jim had everything. A large, beautiful home in the foothills of Tucson. A good family. He ran a great business, played golf every weekend, took great vacations. He had the life we are all shooting for, and all anyone could remember about him was that he sure liked salsa.

As we talked some more, it became clear that Jim passed on a lot of his parenting responsibilities to his wife. That he spent a lot more time on the golf course closing deals than he did at the baseball field with his sons. He failed to teach his daughter how to find a husband and what to look for in a man, and she felt lost in her season of life.

I tell you that story because, of all the things in the book, if you miss this, you will probably end up without breathing room in your life in six months. You can make changes to your schedule, cut something out, change your finances or what you eat, but if you never define *why* you are doing it, you will miss it and change won't be sustained.

Start with Why

A few years ago I read a book that put words to a lot of things I had in my head. It's called *Start with Why* by Simon Sinek (Portfolio, 2009). In it, he showed how the companies that are effective and healthy and reach their mark can tell you *why* they do what they do. He said that most companies can tell you what they do or how they do it, but can rarely tell you why they do something.

It is the same way with churches and families.

Churches talk about all the ministries and programs they have, all the things they offer and do. This class, that choir, this trip, that study. Families can tell you all the things they do and how they do it. Look at their calendar and you will get a clear picture of this.

Where families fall off is that they can't explain *why* they do something.

That's been the point of this whole book: helping us to uncover why we do what we do and seeing if that is where God wants us to be.

That's the goal of this exercise on purpose. I want you personally (and your family, if you have one) to be able to define *why* you do what you do.

The Exercise

Let's get started.[5]

Earlier we considered some things we want to be true about us as we grow older and die. Now that we have a clearer picture of that, let's move on to our kids.

If you have kids, what kind of adults do you want them to be? What do you want them to know? Are there any character qualities you want them to have or avoid? How important is creativity, hard work, integrity, and community to you, just to name a few things? Many parents hope their kids will grow up and need very little counseling and be upstanding citizens. Often, though, we parent so our kids won't embarrass us, or at the very least so they'll make us look good as parents.

We don't parent with goals in an intentional way. Instead, we simply pass on to our kids what we know, what was done to us, or what we see others do.

How long should this list be? As long as you want it to be. At this point, you aren't trying to think of a catchy phrase or a final answer. We'll get to that in a moment.

Now you know what kind of adults you'd like to produce, what you want to be true about you and your kids as you raise them, or your grandkids if you don't have kids in the house anymore. As you look at the things you'd like to be true about your kids or grandkids, are you hitting that mark? If you want your kids to have a servant heart, care for those around them, and have a heart for missions, do you see that in them? Are you giving them an opportunity to accomplish that now? If creativity is something you see in your kids and you want to encourage that, is that happening in your house? Again, without knowing it, we parent out of what we know, what was done to us, and what we see others do. And that isn't always the correct way.

At this point, you should have a list of character traits and qualities you'd like to be true about your family.

Now let's make a second list.

If someone who knows you well were to make a list of qualities describing you and your family, what words would they put on that list? Would they put "laughter," "serving," "creativity," "hospitality"? This list isn't about what you want to be true, but what is true about your family. There might be words on this list that excite you and others that make you cringe. At this point, that is okay. The ones that make you wince are the ones keeping you from the ones that make your heart beat faster, and we need to face both of them. Make this list as exhaustive as possible, because we aren't editing anything yet. Think of a reporter collecting clues.

As you look at your lists, talk about the ones that make you wince. The ones that say, "Our family fights a lot," "We don't eat together," or "We don't have date nights." In this book, we've talked about many of the things that are on that list, and hopefully you have been making notes about how to make changes in those areas. Remember, those are the things that are keeping you from having the breathing room and life God has called you to. They are keeping your family from becoming who God has called them to be.

After you have worked through the wincing list, let's look at the things that are true about you, that make you excited. That list may have words like "organized," "loving," "laughing," "hard work," "creativity," "hospitality," "family," or "serving."

I want to ask you to do something that you will think is very difficult, but it's incredibly important. I want you to pick five words and prepare a family mission statement that centers on them. You want something short enough to put someplace in your house where everyone can see it, and short enough that everyone can memorize it.

I'll give you an example. Here is our family mission statement: *We strive to live a life of gratitude that is a passionate and intentional adventure toward God. With our family at the center, we look for ways to be gracious, generous, and hospitable; learning and laughing all the way.*

I want to ask you to do something when you have your statement. This will be hard, but it's a crucial part of the exercise. I want you to show it to a trusted friend. When we created our mission statement, another couple we are close friends with worked on theirs as well. One night we went out to dinner together and shared our mission statements. The point of this is to get a trusted friend to say, "Yes, that is true about your family," or, "That is not true about your family." If you get a lot of feedback that's the second option, talk about what would have to change to live out the life you feel God is calling you to.

The Most Important Thing Right Now

One of the things that Patrick Lencioni suggests that families do in *The Three Big Questions for a Frantic Family* is to ask, "Over the next three to six months, what is the most important thing for our family to accomplish?" This has been incredibly helpful and liberating for our family. It is easy to look at a book like this and think, "I need to change my schedule, cut things out, get out of debt, work on my health and waistline, let go of things in my past, and deal with hidden sins." It can be overwhelming. And that is just you. When you bring a spouse and kids into the picture, it becomes incredibly daunting. That is why this question is so helpful. What is the most important change you can make right now? What would bring the most freedom to your family and life right now? What would bring the biggest change to your life right now? Sometimes this can last for more than six months or less than three. Debt can take a while to get out of, and so can losing weight, but once the habit is created, I think you can move on to a new one.

This also does something else for you, and it is an important psychological reality: it provides a win.

We all like to win. We all like to feel as if results are happening, especially men. We want to know that the work we are putting in is paying off and moving the ball forward. By looking to a short-term goal like this, you are able to see that something is happening.

Circles of Relationships

Many of us find meaning in our relationships. They shape so much
of our lives. Before we part ways, I want to say one last thing on
relationships. In terms of breathing room, this might be the most
important thing I've said on the subject. We often join groups,
teams, committees, or make volunteer commitments without
much thought. Slowly, our circles of relationships begin growing
to the point that we know many people but lack true community.
I want you to think about every relationship you have (serving
team at church, small group, PTA, children's sports teams, work,
neighbors) as a circle. You will have multiple people in a circle,
but each commitment of community makes up a circle. Even if
you think you don't spend much time with it or you don't have
friends in it, like a child's sports team, it's a circle.

The reality is, your circles all take up time. And as we've seen
so far, there is a limit to the time you have. Each time you add a
new circle or a circle expands because of the commitment that
circle requires, you are pulling away from another circle, and you
only have so much time to go around. Many times, we haphazardly
add circles and then lack community. For men, as we grow older,
this becomes an enormous problem.

While men don't do relationships the way women do them,
we need them just as much. It seems that as men get older,
because of the time they give to their career and their children's
activities, they begin pulling away from friends to the point that
when a man turns forty, he can't think of anyone to call for a beer
or to go fishing.

If that's the case for you, it means you have allowed your circles
to get out of control.

In our family, when we talk about adding a new circle, we also take one away. This limits the number of circles you are a part of. We believe community is that important. And yes, this means we will miss out on things, disappoint people, and even anger people.

Burdens, Community, and Pride

Not only that, but many families and men also struggle to have healthy community with people. In Galatians 6:2 Paul tells us that community should be a place where we carry each other's burdens.

To carry someone's burden, to help with what weighs them down, you have to be close enough to carry it. Many of us do not have anyone close enough to help carry something. This is what I call waiting to build community until you need it. This ensures you will be alone and carry your burden by yourself. You have to build community before you need it, not the other way around. You have to get past your fears, open yourself up to others, and let them in.

What's interesting about Galatians 6 is that Paul says it is possible to sin in two ways:

1. You can sin by not carrying someone else's burden when they need you to.
2. You can sin by not allowing someone to carry your burden when you need them to.

The first one, most people would agree with. When you see someone who needs help, you should help. If you are able to help, do so. If you don't, you are selfish and mean. That point isn't as big an issue, although maybe that is a struggle for you because of pride and selfishness (Gal. 5:25–26).

The second point may be what catches us off guard. What if we try to do it ourselves? What if we never ask for help? What if we never open ourselves up to community and the care others can give us, or allow someone to carry our burden? *We are sinning as much as the selfish, prideful person who won't help.*

Why?

Both have missed community and relationships. Both have pride issues and think they don't need help or others. Both lack humility.

The Impact of Purpose

Is it an overstatement to say that if you don't do this, you'll always be gasping for air? Or that you'll miss life because you won't have healthy relationships?

I don't think so.

Think in terms of a company or a church. When an organization has a clear mission statement, a clear win that everyone knows, so much becomes easier. When a win is defined, a loss is also defined. When someone says, "This is okay," they are also saying, "That is not okay." You are also creating guardrails, and I think that is something many families today lack. If your family does not have a clearly defined purpose, every opportunity your family gets is worth considering, no matter how much it costs or how stressful it will make your life. If the only gauge for a decision is, "Are others doing this? Do I think this will benefit my child?" you will do a number of things you will wish you hadn't. Yes, you want your child to benefit, but not every opportunity does that.

Take our statement that I shared earlier: *We strive to live a life of gratitude that is a passionate and intentional adventure toward*

God. With our family at the center, we look for ways to be gracious,
generous, and hospitable; learning and laughing all the way.

There are a number of things in this statement that drive our family. If you spend any time with our family, you will hear a lot of talk about gratitude. We talk a lot about the needs we have and teach our kids the difference between needs and wants. "Intentional" is another important word for us. We don't do anything haphazardly or by accident. If we are someplace, doing anything, it is because we choose to be. The pressure of being somewhere because we are expected to, or because someone will not approve of us if we aren't there, does not enter our minds. Why? We decided their opinion wasn't as important as being intentional with God in our lives.

"Toward God" is also important. It defines how we will live our lives and which direction we will face, what we will worship and who will be the driver of our lives. We are always before God, always accountable, always reflecting God to the world around us. This dictates how we speak to each other, how we relate, and how we relate to others.

One of the most important statements is "our family at the center." It is important that we do things together as a family, whether that is family dinner, daddy dates, or playing out front. It is also one of the reasons we homeschool as a family; we want our family working together, being together. That isn't the only way to define that phrase, but it is how we have chosen to act it out.

Lastly, there are the five words I mentioned for you to lay out. For us, they are "gracious, generous, hospitable, learning, and laughing."

The order is not accidental. Grace is what drives our lives. It is what has been extended to us by God and what we are called to extend to each other. It dictates how we give grace and second chances to our kids. How we teach them to relate to each other. A common phrase you will hear in our family is "Let's give them grace." Same with "generous." If God is generous with us, as we saw in Chapter Three, we are to be generous with others. We want to hold our possessions loosely. We don't look at our stuff and money the way others do. For example, while planting Revolution Church and going through hard times financially because of that planting, we put five tax refunds toward our adoption and the adoption of friends. Why? We wanted to be generous. It was something we decided described our family and who we wanted to be.

"Hospitable" is another important piece. We want to open our home to others. When friends come over, we want them to love being at our house so they won't want to leave. We want the friends of our kids to come over and think we have the coolest house on the block. Not so our kids will stay home, but because the family is at the center, and we want to be hospitable toward each other and those we welcome into our home.

"Learning and laughing all the way" describes how important learning and growth are. Katie and I model reading in front of our kids, learning about God, arts, theology, and current events, and continually growing. We want our kids to take the posture of being learners, of continually growing, knowing that we never arrive. And lastly, laughter. We want to have fun. We want our house to be filled with giggles and smiles. We want our kids to have fond memories of dance parties in the living room, practicing wrestling moves on the floor, playing surfboard in the pool, and doing plays in the playroom with the dress-up box.

This is *why* our family exists. It drives how we spend our money, how we spend our time, who we are friends with, what activities we sign up for, and which ones we pass up. With this guardrail, we are able to make choices to get us to the place we believe God wants us instead of choices that hinder us. It is the same for your family. When things are more clearly defined, when the win and loss is clarified, when an opportunity comes up, you will have a clearer idea if you should do something instead of asking, "Is everyone else doing it? Does it seem like a good opportunity?"

This gives a clearer idea for you as you think about your goal for the next three to six months. Your goal might not fit my purpose, and vice versa. I had a mentor tell me that when you have a clear mission and purpose, that one decision erases the need to make the next hundred decisions. It also brings clarity to your circles of relationships. Our family is involved in many of our relationships. We want to be friends with our children's friends and their parents. While I do things with other men without my kids, I often involve them in what I do. Why? Because I want our family at the center, and we've already decided this is important.

Sustaining New Life

This is important because, as John Ortberg said, "For Jesus, identity and acceptance come before achievement and ministry. This is joy no one can take away. You cannot earn acceptance."[6] Until you believe and know that you are fully loved by God, a son or daughter who has been bought through the redemption of Jesus by his death and resurrection, you will find yourself running from one thing to the next. Always looking for something that isn't there, but which seems to be just out of your reach. Longing for approval you will never find apart from Jesus. Fearing silence that doesn't have to be scary, because Jesus is there.

When we know this, when we live in this, we are able to sustain new life.

This is the last crucial step to breathing room.

When I lost 130 pounds, my friends and family were excited, but there is always skepticism when someone loses a bunch of weight, gets out of debt, or makes a big change in their lives. We wait for them to put it back on, get into more debt, or make a poor decision. Our skepticism is often warranted, as many people fall back into old ways.

The reasoning is simple: it is what we know, and we are comfortable in what we know. There will be moments in your future when you will find yourself returning to an uncontrollable schedule, eating an unsustainable diet, or spending money you don't have to impress people you don't like.

When you feel tempted, remember the work we've done together. Remember the plates that we have pulled off, the sin under the sin we have discovered, and the freedom that Jesus holds out to you and says is yours when you are in him.

It is tempting in our world to live like everybody else does. To run at the pace they run and fill our calendars in hopes of having the good life. But after all that we've walked through together, you know that you don't want to go back to the way it was, to what you've known.

When Paul makes a plea in the book of Galatians to the churches who are going back to their old ways, believing in law and good works instead of trusting in the grace of God, Paul essentially tells them, "Now that you are free and have experienced freedom, why would you go back?"[7]

That's my final encouragement to you. Once you have breathed new air and have experienced the freedom that comes from being in Jesus and having breathing room, why would you go back to that slavery, to that pace, that debt or those addictions?

Breathing New Air

This is the last "Breathing New Air."

I don't want us to miss anything we've worked on so far. It would be tempting to try to change everything in your life right now. It's tempting to try to tackle our imaginary world, addictions, debt, schedule and pace, weight and eating habits, or how we see ourselves. Few people can tackle all those things at the same time. Realistically, let's talk about three immediate things you can do. For each reader, what those things are and how those things need to change will be different.

Discussion Questions

1. How has your search for meaning kept you from having *breathing room?*

2. Explain how you have seen this truth played out in your life: *Your system is perfectly designed to give you the results you are getting.*

3. How has your view of *breathing room* and the possibility of having it in your life changed over the course of this book?

4. As we wrap up our time together, if you haven't already created a family or personal mission statement, now is the time to do that.

Endnotes

Chapter 1

[1] Andy Stanley, "Breathing Room: Time" (sermon given at North Point Community Church, Alpharetta, Georgia, January 13, 2013).

Chapter 2

[1] Dean Obeidallah, "Take Your Vacation, or Die?" *CNN*, July 15, 2012, accessed November 9, 2012, http://www.cnn.com/2012/07/13/opinion/obeidallah-vacation-health/index.html.

[2] Ibid.

[3] Ideas, in part, drawn from a WebMD feature, "How to Get a Good Night's Sleep," MedicineNet.com, January 30, 2005, accessed November 10, 2012, http://www.medicinenet.com/script/main/art.asp?articlekey=50595.

[4] David Murray, "50 Good Reasons to Sleep Longer," HeadHeartHand Blog, May 14, 2014, accessed May 27, 2014, http://headhearthand.org/blog/2014/05/14/arrogance-of-ignoring-our-need-of-sleep/.

[5] Mark Buchanan, *The Rest of God: Restoring Your Soul by Restoring Sabbath* (Nashville: Thomas Nelson, 2006), 3.

[6] Andy Stanley, "Breathing Room: Time" (sermon given at North Point Community Church, Alpharetta, Georgia, January 13, 2013).

[7] Buchanan, *The Rest of God*, 129.

Chapter 3

[1] Andy Stanley, "Breathing Room: Dollars and Sense" (sermon given at North Point Community Church, Alpharetta, Georgia, January 20, 2013).

[2] "Americans in Debt," Debt.org, accessed June 18, 2014, http://www.debt.org/faqs/americans-in-debt/.

[3] To hear a sermon on this, go to http://www.tucsonrevolution .com/sermon/change-living-like-a-child-of-god-galatians-326-47.

[4] Two of my favorites are *The Total Money Makeover* by Dave Ramsey (Thomas Nelson, 2003) and *Smart Couples Finish Rich* by David Bach (Crown Business, 2002).

[5] Luke 18:22.

[6] Andy Stanley, "Breathing Room: Time" (sermon given at North Point Community Church, Alpharetta, Georgia, January 13, 2013).

[7] Matthew 6:25–34 ESV.

Chapter 4

[1] "New Year's Resolution Statistics," Statistic Brain, January 26, 2015, http://www.statisticbrain.com/new-years-resolution-statistics/.

[2] "Overweight and Obesity: Adult Obesity Facts," Centers for Disease Control and Prevention, last modified September 9, 2014, http://www.cdc.gov/obesity/data/adult.html.

[3] "Obesity Statistics: 42% of America Obese by 2030," *Inquisitr,* May 8, 2012, http://www.inquisitr.com/231930/obesity-statistics-42-percent -of-americans-obese-by-2030/.

[4] "Overweight & Obesity Statistics," U.S. Department of Health and Human Services, updated October 2012, http://win.niddk.nih.gov /publications/PDFs/stat904z.pdf.

[5] "Overweight and Obesity: Economic Consequences," Centers for Disease Control and Prevention, last modified April 27, 2012, http:// www.cdc.gov/obesity/adult/causes/index.html.

[6] "Statistical Fact Sheet: Overweight and Obesity, 2013 Update," American Heart Association, http://www.heart.org/idc/groups /heart-public/@wcm/@sop/@smd/documents/downloadable/ucm _319588.pdf.

[7] "Overweight Children in America—Childhood Obesity Statistics," Ygoy Health Community, http://obesity.ygoy.com/overweight -children-in-america-childhood-obesity-statistics/.

[8] American Heart Association, http://www.heart.org/idc/groups /heart-public/@wcm/@fc/documents/downloadable/ucm _428180.pdf.

[9] My wife and I preached a sermon together on body image that might be helpful, which you can find at http://www.tucsonrevolution.com/sermon/beautiful-me-beautiful-genesis-126-27/.

[10] "11 Facts About Body Image," DoSomething.org, accessed July 7, 2015, https://www.dosomething.org/facts/11-facts-about-body-image.

[11] Genesis 1:26–27 ESV.

[12] 1 Corinthians 6:12, 19–20 ESV.

[13] Scott Stoll, MD, "Fat in Church," FoxNews.com, January 4, 2013, accessed November 9, 2012, http://www.foxnews.com/opinion/2012/06/03/obesity-epidemic-in-america-churches/.

[14] Ibid.

[15] If you are curious about how I exercise, you can find that information here: http://joshuareich.org/2013/11/25/how-to-do-crossfit-on-your-own/.

[16] This choice is more about an intolerance than a desire to not eat wheat.

[17] If you'd like some ideas on how I eat, you can read this: http://joshuareich.org/2012/07/18/what-i-eat/.

Chapter 5

[1] Peggy Fletcher Stack, "Utah Faith Leaders Battle the Hidden Sin: Porn Addiction," *Salt Lake Tribune,* November 25, 2011, accessed May 27, 2014, http://www.sltrib.com/sltrib/lifestyle/52874266-80/anderson-porn-pornography-says.html.csp.

[2] "Can Romance Novels Hurt Your Heart," Moore to the Point, May 18, 2011, http://www.russellmoore.com/2011/05/18/can-romance-novels-hurt-your-heart/.

[3] While porn is often seen as an issue only men struggle with, it is also a struggle for many women. I asked a woman who struggled with this issue to write a blog post about her struggle and how she found freedom. You can read that blog here: http://joshuareich.org/2015/04/24/when-a-woman-struggles-with-a-mans-problem/.

[4] "Addiction," *Gale Encyclopedia of Medicine* as cited in The Free Dictionary, http://medical-dictionary.thefreedictionary.com/addiction.

⁵Kate Shellnutt, "What People Gave Up for Lent 2013 (According to Twitter)," *Christianity Today* Gleanings, February 18, 2013, www.christianitytoday.com/gleanings/2013/february/what-people-gave-up-for-lent-2013-according-to-twitter.html.

⁶Ephesians 5:22–33.

Chapter 6

¹Greg McKeown, *Essentialism: The Disciplined Pursuit of Less* (New York: Crown, 2014), 12.

²Ibid.

³Peter Drucker interview with Bruce Rosenstein on April 11, 2005. Bruce wrote up the interview in his book *Living in More Than One World: How Peter Drucker's Wisdom Can Inspire and Transform Your Life* (San Francisco: Berrett-Koehler, 2009).

⁴Tim Chester, "The 4Gs—truths to set you free," September 1, 2009, http://timchester.wordpress.com/2009/09/01/the-4gs-truths-to-set-you-free/.

Chapter 8

¹Timothy Keller, *The Wedding Party* (New York: Penguin, 2013).

²Jeremiah 31:31–34, 33:10–11.

³Hosea 2:16–20.

⁴Amos 9:11–15.

⁵Timothy Keller, *Jesus the King* (New York: Penguin, 2013).

⁶Tim Chester, "The 4Gs—truths to set you free," September 1, 2009, http://timchester.wordpress.com/2009/09/01/the-4gs-truths-to-set-you-free/.

Chapter 9

¹Timothy Keller, *Walking with God through Pain and Suffering* (New York: Penguin, 2013), 13.

Chapter 10

¹"W. Edwards Deming," Wikipedia, last modified April 13, 2015, http://en.wikipedia.org/wiki/W._Edwards_Deming.

[2]Henry T. Blackaby and Richard Blackaby, *Spiritual Leadership: Moving People on to God's Agenda* (Nashville: B & H Publishing, 2001), 193.

[3]Brad Lomenick, *The Catalyst Leader: 8 Essentials for Becoming a Change Maker* (Nashville: Thomas Nelson, 2013), 21.

[4]Not his real name.

[5]Patrick Lencioni's book *The Three Big Questions for a Frantic Family* (Jossey-Bass, 2008) has been incredibly helpful in my thinking on this exercise.

[6]John Ortberg, *Soul Keeping: Caring for the Most Important Part of You* (Grand Rapids: Zondervan, 2014), 127.

[7]Galatians 4:8–9.